Breaking Through!

WOMEN SURVIVING MALE VIOLENCE

Published by the Women's Aid Federation England Ltd.
© W.A.F.E. Ltd. 1989
ISBN: 0 907817 30 0

Copies available from:
W.A.F.E. Ltd.
P.O. Box 391
Bristol BS99 7WS

Cartoons by Rae Sibbitt and others
Cover illustration by Christine Smith
Typeset and printed by:
Sheffield Women's Printing Co-op (TU) Ltd. (0742) 753180

CONTENTS

ACKNOWLEDGEMENTS

We would like to thank the Preparatory Educational Project – an Adult Education programme run jointly by Ruskin College, Workers Educational Association (Bucks., Berks., and Oxon region), and the Open University, (Southern region), for having the imagination to support the work which we did together to write this book. Through their assistance, we were able to meet on a regular basis with paid facilitators/tutors, both in our own home town but also in two memorable but exhausting residential weekends at Ruskin College. Not only did their financial support (which also covered Educational resource materials, childcare and transport costs) enable us to work together as a group in a way that would not otherwise have been possible, but we were also supported by their belief that ours was an "educational group" – that we could use our experience for our own learning and for that of others.

We would also like to thank the Women's Aid Federation (England) for agreeing to publish *"Breaking Through"*, and feel that it is particularly appropriate as several women in the group have lived and also worked in Women's Aid refuges. We have been influenced by the thinking of many women in the Women's Aid movement, especially in the "What causes the Violence" chapter – but of course the views expressed in the book are our own rather than claiming to represent the views of other women in Women's Aid.

Our thanks also to the Sheffield Women's Printing Co-op for the patience they have shown in sorting out our manuscript and fitting in our last minute illustrations and alterations.

Lastly, we would like to give a very warm "thank you" to Rae Sibbitt, who came in at a very late stage of the project to help us to put our ideas on illustrating the book into reality. Also to one or two of our artistic daughters and sons – we've always specially liked the picture of the woman going to the toilet in peace on page 91! Violence against women is not a humorous subject, but as well as sharing a lot of our pain within the group we have also always laughed a lot. We hope that the cartoons will help readers share our feeling of energy and optimism in at last making the break.

HOW TO USE THIS BOOK

This book has been written by and for women who are experiencing male violence – or who have suffered from it in the past. We also hope that anyone who might be in contact with women experiencing male violence – which is practically everyone – will learn from reading it.

We hope that it is all worth reading, but it doesn't have to be read in any particular order.

If you need immediate help there are a list of useful phone numbers at the back of the book. Chapters 5 and 6 may also be helpful because they describe our experience in going for help – and chapter 6 in particular talks about what Women's Aid refuges can offer.

Chapters 1-3 discuss the violence itself – and are possibly the most depressing parts of the book. We have found comfort in learning that we were not alone in the violence we have suffered, though, and hope that other women will find our writing helps them to break out of the feeling that they are "the only one this is happening to".

Chapter 4 looks at some of the common explanations of male violence towards women – and says what we think is at the root of the problem. We think that this is an important chapter because until we understand what is happening, we cannot fight it – either for ourselves or for other women. We refer back to it a lot in chapters 5-10. Perhaps the most important thing that it says is that it is NOT WOMEN WHO ARE TO BLAME.

The last part of the book – chapters 7-10 are about our experience and thoughts on surviving male violence. We look at our own lives and the lives of our children, and the choices open to us. Although we do not under-estimate the difficulties of making a new start – we hope that this is the most hopeful part of the book, and will at least start other women thinking about some of the choices open to them.

Sometimes we would "brainstorm" a long list of ideas

INTRODUCTION

Who are we?

We are a group of women who have all (but one) experienced violence from men either as children or adults — or both. The violence has taken a number of forms — physical, sexual and mental, and sometimes all three. We came together to write this book — which was the first writing some of us had done since leaving school.

We are a very varied group — Londoners, first and second generation Irish women, Englishwomen, one black Jamaican woman, one Scottish and one Welsh woman. Some do paid work, others work unpaid at home. Most of us have children, and are single parents.

We have a range of religious and political beliefs — and attitudes towards men — but all believe in women having more choice over how they live their lives.

How have we gone about writing the book?

When we got together as a group of women, all of us had ideas about what should go into the book and what we felt would be useful to other women who might be going through some sort of violence.

Over many weeks we all got together. We talked a lot about the way we felt that violence had affected us, and what we could do to help ourselves and others. We would decide on a topic, or a couple at a time and split up into smaller groups. Sometimes some of us would go away and write what they themselves had experienced. Sometimes we would tape what we talked about, at other times we would "brainstorm" a long list of ideas about a particular topic. Anything we wrote, we brought back to the group, and some pieces were written and rewritten.

Sometimes we found it very stressful, as it went very deeply into our own personal lives. Together as a group we were able to discuss our feelings freely. This helped us to come to terms with our lives, helping us to grow day by day a lot stronger, putting the past behind us, growing for the future, knowing we have overcome our fears, knowing that through all our hard work we are helping someone overcome theirs.

What else has happened to us while we were writing the book?

Working on the book was having a strong effect on our lives and emotions, and women often brought this back to the group to be talked about. A lot of things happened to the women in the group in the year that we met; one woman has had a baby; some women have got new jobs; two women have been raped — and one had an abortion; two girl children have been sexually abused; relationships have been affected by the group, and some have broken up — whilst others have developed in positive ways. Some of what has happened has acted as a grim reminder of the reality of male violence, and how common it is, both in and outside the home.

As a group — now of very close friends — it has been important to give each other support and love.

What's missing from the book?

It took months before we really got writing — looking back, most of us didn't feel very confident about putting pen to paper. But then, when we did, we found that we had more and more to say. When we at last had a draft copy of "the book", we began thinking again — about all the important things we had left out of it. Some things we added at the last moment, but there is still a lot left out. For example, we haven't written much about how a woman's experience of violence is affected by her class, her sexuality, or her cultural background. In the end too, we still felt that the book was more depressing than we would like, and didn't stress enough the positive things which women can achieve when they work together to say "NO" to violence.

The effect the group has had on us

We would like to finish our introduction with a list written by all of us on the effects which the group has had on us.

— *Made us depressed, sad, and frightened.*

— *Given us awareness, strength, security, care and love.*

— *Opened our eyes — and made us angry about male violence.*

— *Given us the energy to want to do something about it.*

— *Helped us to face reality and to feel it — that has been painful — but at least we're more alive.*

— *Given us the space and safety to share our feelings and experience and to work things through .*

— *Made us more open to other women's choices — sexuality, lifestyle etc.*

— *Helped us to believe what has happened to us :*

"Because half the time when I look back I think "I couldn't have gone through all that — it's just a big story" — but then you listen to other people, and you find that they've been through it as well."

— *Made us more aware of what causes men to be violent to women — and of how much there is in our society which encourages them.*

— *Stopped us blaming ourselves.*

If women reading this book stop blaming themselves for the violence that they receive from men, if it encourages them to consider leaving violent relationships, and to look for the support they need in order to "make the break" then it will have been worth writing.

We would like to dedicate this book to every woman who has experienced violence — with love from all of us.

CHAPTER ONE:
MENTAL, PHYSICAL AND SEXUAL VIOLENCE

In this chapter we write about the different forms of violence we have experienced as adult women. We hope that women reading this will see that if they are suffering from similar treatment, they are not alone — *that it is not their fault* — and that they don't have to put up with it.

Some of us have also experienced violence as children — expecially sexual violence. We see this as part of an overall problem of male violence towards women, and write about it in chapter 3.

PHYSICAL VIOLENCE

My husband was violent to myself and the children, particularly in our first year of marriage, and also sometimes before marriage.

Before my first child was born and I was pregnant I can remember being thumped and having bruises on my arms and legs. The nurse at the maternity clinic did ask me if I bruised easily, I said "Yes"; she did not ask me how, and I did not tell her. Although I had a feeling my husband could be violent, I did not know or realise what living with violence would be like and if I had thought about it more before being married, I would not have got married. My first year was hell. Sunday afternoons were the worst times, after lunchtime drinking sessions, and I always felt very nervy and tense. In the beginning I used to fight back, but later on it seemed that if I didn't retaliate he didn't hurt as much. He was just in a bad temper one night and kicked and kicked my legs and I had lots of bruises down them. One Sunday afternoon when my first baby was just a few months old we were arguing and he hit me in the face and split the underneath of my lip. I had to have a doctor and he put a stitch in and the scar is still there, also one of my bottom teeth is crooked because he chipped it. He would punch the children from a few months old, and I left him when my first was five months old. But he came round to see us and said he was sorry and we went back. I had complained to the court and he had to go to court, but because we were back at home he was given probation.

Things improved a bit after that but when the baby was seven months old I left again and the same happened again. I brought charges again and he was put on probation for another term. After the first year of my marriage the violence subsided to the odd punch on me but he was always 'strict', mean and cruel to the kids. This makes it very difficult to cope with the oldest now, who was more often picked on than the younger one who wasn't treated quite so harshly. The oldest is more aggressive, and 'difficult' and unfortunately will probably, unless he has an understanding wife, show violence. He used to tell me he would not beat his wife like his dad did. Now myself and my kids live without so much stress, they do relax more, and have most likely forgotten a lot of the things we put up with as I think I have, until just sometimes I remember and know that I would not go through all that again. I have had black eyes etc. and the boys have had some bruising. It is not always something you wanted to talk about.

Philippa

You say you love me
You say you care
You say you hit me
    'cos ask for it I dare
When you say "do it"
    you expect me to jump
Your mistakes and wrongs I'm
    expected to accept
I'm allowed no mistakes
I'm allowed no wrongs.

You say I'm deaf
You say I'm thick
You say I'm stupid
You say I'm a fucking bitch
You say you tell me what
    I should do and say
You say if I did, you wouldn't
    treat me this way
You say I ask for it
You say it's my fault
You say you love me
You say you care.

You say what you want
    what clothes and what toys
You get what you want
    your clothes and your toys
You say you have needs
    which you will get fulfilled
You say you love me
You say you care.

I reckon you're selfish
too selfish to love
too selfish to care
You love yourself, your needs
    and your toys

There's one toy that's gone
gone for good and for keeps
gone from your shelf
gone from your reach
because it needs love
because it needs care
yet you say you love me
  you say you care.

Sylvia

I don't respect the way you bully
I don't respect the way you shout
I don't respect the way you take
and watch others go without

I don't respect the way you treat us
your need to be dominant, authoritarian, and big-mouthed
I don't respect how you talk to us
belittling us, overpowering us
  and all so very loud

I've wanted you to turn and see
what effect it all has had on me
I've let you do it for so long
now our time has come and gone.

Sylvia

A violent incident which happened

My husband's niece came to visit us one evening and stayed to dinner. At this time (which was a usual occurrence) my husband was not talking to me at all. His niece who was studying at college got into a heated discussion with my husband on foreigners living in this country. She was friendly with her colleagues of mixed races but my husband would not listen to any of her points of view, only his views. She left our house very upset.

I did not enter into the discussion at all but tried to calm her down because she was upset. On going to bed that evening my husband accused me of taking her side against him, which was not true. I replied that he was not always right. He straight away lashed out at me and hit me around the bedroom using his fists, he then kicked me down the stairs shouting abuse all the time. We ended up in the living room, me sitting on the settee shaking, him standing in front with his fist clenched. I remember saying "I'm scared of you" and he just replied "I know". With that he dropped his fist and appeared to calm down. After drinking coffee I said I would like to sleep in the spare room which he agreed to (which was unusual).

This particular incident sticks in my mind because although I only suffered a black eye and bruises to legs and arms it was three days later when looking straight at me during dinner he saw my eye and realised what he had done. He apologised and said he didn't know he had hit me. As it turned out he never hit me again but it really scared me that he didn't know what he had done and I finally realised what sort of person I was living with and I was not at fault.

Mavis

Dot and Elaine talking about their experience of violence

Dot. *It gets more frequent doesn't it, the gaps between the violence get shorter.*

Elaine. Yes, it gets so you think they are planning it. You can feel the tension building up — that's what was happening before I left.

D. *Then you got out at a good time!*

E. I used to get really frightened when he went out drinking and then I'd hear the key in the door, about half 11 and you'd think — this is it — and he'd be blinking drunk and that would be nearly every night, and if he didn't have the money to drink he'd nick it out of my purse anyway.

D. *In the end my husband didn't need a drink to do it — he'd do it in the middle of the street — anywhere.*

E. It never got to the stage where mine would do that.

D. *Mine got really bad.*

E. Mind he threw an egg at me in the middle of Waitrose all over my face. *(Laughed)* He had to pay for it in the end.

D. *What did you say — How do you like your eggs, fried or boiled?*

E. Everyone just looked. I thought "Oh come on swallow me ground. I did laugh, but I didn't think it was really funny — I was really hysterical!

Every time the key went in the door my heart was in my mouth, I was alright during the day. One day he asked me to post a letter — I couldn't find it. When I couldn't find it he hit me — but he had purposely put it in the junk cupboard in a little brown box just as an excuse.

He never bought anything for my daughter — not even a Christmas present. I think it might have been because he married late. I never saw his wage packet. I remember the Sunday before we went into the refuge, they had had to have hula hoops for their dinner and I had the leftovers.

One morning he got up while we were having breakfast, and I said "You can make it yourself for a change" and he went to boil this egg, and the shell went into his mouth, he threw them both across the room and they landed on the cupboard and they looked like two knockers. I had my face in my hands trying not to laugh, and then he made himself a cup of tea and the sugar bowl was too near the edge of the cup and it fell down — that annoyed him. Then without thinking he took the cup of tea to his mouth and it didn't have sugar or milk in. And then he burnt his toast under the grill . . . and then he threw a knife at me, and it just dug into the door. I got out and when I came back the next day after he had calmed down he had thrown all my clothes out and put mud on top of them. That was one incident when I had to laugh, but it was fatal to let him see me laugh because it made him worse. I didn't have to let him see me cry — because that's what he wanted.

Extracts from Elizabeth's story

In .... I met my second husband. Right from the start we had a good sexual relationship, learned a lot about our needs together; we used to spend most of our time in bed together. Our relationship was now I realise only sexual because, when the sex stopped so our marriage fell apart. He had been violent right from the start, but I used to pretend things would get better. I always blamed myself for being so outspoken, but when I had my first daughter and he turned on me I knew he was at fault, not me. On good days he had a habit of poking a finger in my rib cage or sitting on top of me with his head against mine or keeping me looking at him while he spoke.

15

What really got to me after seven years was when he was home after the night shift he would go up to bed and he would tell me to come up when he called because I had to perform my duty. He used to want sex at least twice a day or he would get mad. After the birth of my son I completely hated him and made all excuses. I had had a difficult birth and had to have stitches. I bled for three months and he was getting frustrated and started to knock me about.

My son (my third child) wasn't planned and my husband told me to have an abortion, but I knew I couldn't go through with it and for the first time stood up to him.

For nine months I went through hell. My husband did everything he could to make me unhappy. At times he never spoke, just sat watching the television. He was very cold towards me — the only time he came close was when he wanted sex. I couldn't always give in as I just went off him and every time he came near I used to freeze.

If I had been out to friends he would act as if I was a child and would say I had enough to do in the house and didn't have enough time to call on friends and relations. I knew the house had had a clean and the meal was always on time. With a 20 month old and a 32 month old I needed to get away from the house.

When our son was born he was a very proud father, but this didn't last . . . . He had shut me out of his life for the past nine months and in return I grew to shut him out of mine.

When I returned home I found it hard to cope with three small children . . . . I had a close friend who came around every day, but I used to have to put up with him shouting at me because she had cleaned the house and helped to prepare the dinner. He would throw things around and tell me "I said if you had another you wouldn't be able to cope — you should have got rid of him." Before I sat down to feed my son I would ask him if he wanted coffee or anything — also get the girls settled. Just as my son would start to feed he would pull him away, throw him in his pram and ask me to make him a decent cup of coffee, or say that his dinner wasn't right, and I would have to start all over again.

One night he did this, so I stopped and put my son down. The baby was crying, my husband was shouting, the girls were screaming — I just didn't know which way to turn. I just shouted "I've had enough", tears running down my face. He grabbed hold of me, started to shake me, saying, "Shut those kids up, get my dinner." (I'd already cooked it once.) What was I

16

to do first? I can remember I felt very weak and dazed and not knowing which way to turn. I went to get past him and he hit me, saying I was a fat slut, unfit mother and wife, saying the house was in a mess — saying all that he could. I flew up the stairs into the bathroom, locked myself in thinking he would leave me alone. I lay on the floor crying, then bang, the door flew open. He fell on top of me and started thumping me. I screamed out — he put his hands around my neck, and I passed out for a few seconds. I remember I came back as if I had just woken up. I couldn't cry any longer, I couldn't even say anything to him — he was just looking at me, really frightened. I think he knew he could have killed me. I walked down the stairs, picked up my son, and two daughters and took them into the living room. I started to feed my very hungry son who had tears running down his face — his little hands around my breast. I felt a love for this tiny person, also for my two daughters who were close by my side. I knew then that they were special and they would always come first.

In the meantime, my husband had gone over to friends. I phoned up the doctor, explaining that I couldn't go on any longer, and he said he would phone me back, which he did, but I was too scared to leave.

My husband came back with our "friends". The wife got me on my own, and told me I had let myself go, and the home, and that I was not looking after the kids. She had one child, her home was always in a mess. I was the tidy one while I only had two, but with three I just couldn't find the time. I didn't take any notice — the house was in a mess, my hair was untidy and I was overweight, but I knew I was looking after the kids. I also had a cut and swollen face — but she didn't ask about that!

Elizabeth

Extracts from Janet's story

I *have experienced physical and mental violence throughout my childhood, my early teens and early twenties. My mother had eight children including two sets of twins with 17 months between. She had four children before my twin sister and I were born, three months early. Within that year she buried her first child and my brother's twin. Two years later my mother's father died. These were the most stressful years for her. I don't remember, but she admits to smacking us a lot. I remember from the age of five my father hitting us all with a leather belt late at night, because we were messing about and having pillow fights.*

This physical violence continued until the age of 12 when I left home — my twin sister left three weeks later. During these seven years my mother smacked, kicked, punched and pinched us all, but me and my sister must have been the boldest for we seemed to get it most. My father's violence increased to hitting with the buckle of the belt and steel heels on his shoes. Sometimes if my mum had a bad day with us when my dad came home she would go on about us to him so much that he'd run up the stairs with his belt and lose his temper — sometimes we would be asleep. I look like my mum and she resented that in me, because she didn't like herself much, and when she and my dad rowed, he would single me out and say horrible things to me, say I was just like her. I'd cry a lot — she did too. He treated my twin a little better because she looked like him. When I was seven my mum had a new daughter so the three of us looked alike and were subjected to the same.

As a result of the childhood violence I went into my teens feeling inadequate, very insecure, guilty and totally submissive, not liking myself much, feeling worthless, frightened, and hating my father. I was in a mess emotionally and I felt broken down.

At 16 I met my husband and carried all these feelings into that relationship. He was my first boyfriend. I never loved him, but because of my Catholic upbringing and conditioning I felt I ought to go along with him. He offered me an opportunity to go to Scotland, which to me seemed like America, and besides I wanted out of Ireland. I totally trusted him with my life, I thought he could sort me out because he was 14 years my senior and a social worker, so I decided to make a go out of the relationship.

Within a short time he was physically and sexually abusing me. My father had done this to my mum so I thought this was what life was about. As for the sexual abuse — well I had no previous sexual education and I didn't know it was abuse. So I thought if I had a baby he would not abuse me. I was wrong — he got worse. At first I tried to fight back and answer back, but he was stronger mentally, physically and verbally, so I learned to shut up. He put me down so much, I didn't want to live.

I decided to have my son but he raped me on my two girls. On my first daughter he hurt he most and because of this I resented her a lot. When I was pregnant with my second girl I started to get stronger, and tried to make decisions to try and get away. By this time I was completely terrified of him. Two months before my second daughter was born, he got a job 70 miles away so he was only home at weekends. I'd learned to be strong during the week and started to live independently from him, but I wasn't very successful at this because he was hurting me at weekends when he came. This went on for 18 months. Then one final violent incident came when he tortured me, physically beat me, sexually assaulted and nearly killed me and I left without my kids because I felt I did not want to die then. My willingness to live gave me the strength to leave, not because I was physically hurt, but because

I eventually saw through him and myself. I thought I'm only 23 years old and I realised none of it was right — not him, not for the kids, and it was certainly not the life I wanted. After leaving I learned he had sexually assaulted my girl.

Janet

SEXUAL VIOLENCE

My mother never explained about sex when I was a teenager. I always regretted this, but I feel things may have been different during my marriage if only she could have talked to me about sex.

I was a virgin when I got married. I thought our sex life was going to be something special from conversations I'd had with other people. I was very disappointed. I never reached an orgasm during the nine years we were married. I felt it put a lot of pressure on me.

During his physical and verbal abuse at me on many occasions I was accused of being no good in bed. He started to make me dress up in suspenders, stockings and shoes which obviously aroused him. I was hoping he would try to give me good feelings also. I was very upset when he forced my mouth open for oral sex. I felt really sick. It's not what I wanted or expected. I didn't enjoy it.

He always liked a drink. After drinking he would try to have intercourse with me but because he was not sober he could not come. Parts of my body were very sore because he would not admit defeat. Sometimes I cried because he would not get off me; I prayed he would finish and be satisfied.

On some occasions he touched my body continually for hours leaving me very sore and with no good feelings towards sex. Sometimes spraying my body with sperm — I felt DIRTY. I was too scared to tell anyone or approach him that I didn't like what was happening.

Dot

Take a lodger

Take a lodger, a lodger, they say.
It will be a bit extra, a few pennies more.
Living on Social, not much good.
Three kids and bills, maybe I should.
Yes I decide, I'll give it a try.
Do laundry and food, but clothes I can't dry.
This is the day Mister should come.
Sounds polite on the phone miss's and all.
Tidy the room, he sees at five.
Bright as a pin all ready for Clive.
Wrapping the presents as everything should.
Kids in the garden, I feel so good.
Knock on the door Mister is there.
Stands in a suit shakes hands and smiles.
Being so well mannered, he excuses his wife,
Not well he says, but I think probably a fight.
I take him upstairs to view the room.
Not much I say, hope it will do,
Yes, he says, it's just what I want.
It has a nice view.
Then
As I move he knocks me down.
Produces a knife to keep me down.
I've lost my voice, I cannot scream.
The horror I feel is no dream.
For I know it's too late, he's going to rape.
To him it's a game, I know for sure.
For me a nightmare, the pain no cure.
Kid's in the garden, I'm frightened he'll hear.
Must be silent so much fear.
Now that he's gone I lie quite still.
I've paid the price, to pay the bills.

Janet

MENTAL VIOLENCE

The mental violence I have experienced, destroyed my trust and made me totally insecure.

I have since realised that "the nagging" was all my defence mechanism. There were days when I was told I was mad. My parents were judged according to his. My values were scoffed at. My intelligence was laughed at and those who had it were considered "stupid".

There were blatant lies, cover ups and "hidden truths" as he called them. He told me once that he was afraid of me and how I would react, if I knew the truth.

Any programmes that I watched, for example drama, educational or documentary were called rubbish and football, Benny Hill or Tom and Jerry were preferred.

Any consideration for others was thrown in my face — "If you thought more of me than you do of others". My religion was laughed at. "Only joking" was his pet phrase, "You know me — I didn't mean it" when it had already cut me deep. Tears were my weakness, it's a problem when I try to express anger.

I blamed myself for everything, even though I made it clear, day in and day out that he was to blame.

I felt laughed at behind doors by his workmates and felt I was being called "that miserable bitch".

Sex was virtually non-existent. Because of the way I was treated, mentally, during the day, it was impossible to show affection at night.

Why do I still think and say that I'm just as much to blame? I nagged, I told him he was useless (which he still is). I fought, or so I say, to keep the marriage going. Guilt must not weigh you down. I'm now able to say it is "his problem not mine"!

Then I felt no one could help me, no one could understand, how could I explain to someone who didn't know him? How could I have grounds for a divorce?

Was it all me!! I went to a psychiatrist, I broke down to my husband one night and said I had to get myself sorted out. The psychiatrist said there was nothing wrong with me, that I wasn't mad and all we needed was

Marriage Guidance. He wouldn't go and said it was nobody else's business.

He wouldn't let me inside, he wouldn't let me get really close. He couldn't talk about sex or death and I still don't understand him.

He can't live life for himself — everyone else, wife, parents and friends have to tell him, show him, or live it for him! He twisted me round in circles, twisted what I'd said or told me that I'd told him something, when I hadn't. He really had me believing I was cracking up! I began injuring myself, without feeling any pain at all. I felt like I was trapped and had no escape.

He gambled away our money, left all the bills to me and stole the rent money. He couldn't hold a job, packing it in without notice and sometimes not bothering to even get up to go to work. I used to beg him to try to be responsible and make a future for us. I'd cry all the time at the hundreds of promises that were broken time after time.

Susan

I find this very hard to write about, because in my case I was rather wiped out as a person. My husband is rather overpowering and every time I ever wanted to live my way or have my own opinion he used to get very aggressive in his manner and bully me. In the end I used to back down in most things because if I got my own way he would sulk or take it out ont he children. He only ever hit me once but I feel that was mainly because I never stood up to him — always playing safe. I have always been frightened of violence. I think this goes back to my childhood where the men in the house were always rowing and fighting with each other and I always tried to have my nose in a book or keep a low profile. They say fight or flight. I don't think I even recognised what I was doing because you sure can kid yourself the reasons why you do some things. I don't think things would have got so bad if I had not got such a low opinion of myself.

The one time it did turn into physical violence, it was the most embarrassing thing that has ever happened to me in my life. I know that sounds pretty silly to say. I wasn't scared so much, as embarrasssed, because of where it was and how to deal with it, how to react . . . I couldn't just storm out or run out, because I was in the middle of London with three children and in my mother's front room. And the action of all the people around me was so embarrassing as well. My mother turned the TV up, my stepfather went to make a cup of tea, and there was just this embarrassing silence, you know, 'cause he hit me. You can't react with three children. You don't have a choice, with three little children, in the middle of London, with no money.

Caroline

22

Contraction

During our marriage we alternated between the pill and the sheath. My husband preferred me being on the pill but it always gave me quite bad depression, and from time to time we agreed that I should not take it for a bit. Then the year before he left he started refusing to use the sheath any more; he had always refused to have a vasectomy. I went to the Family Planning Clinic to ask to go on the pill again, but because of my age and the depression the pill caused they refused to prescribe it, neither could I have the coil as my periods were too heavy. This left the cap, and so I was fitted with one of these. I practised putting it in and taking it out but felt very nervous in case I did it wrong. My hands shook as I put it in. I worried all month in case I had done it wrong and got myself pregnant. Then, when my period was due, I did not come on. My husband 'phoned me from work two or three times every day to see if I had started. Every time I had to tell him no. Then early one morning when I was over a week late he came up to the bedroom and said that if I was pregnant he would leave, that I had ruined his life. I stood up and my period flooded.

He was happy again but then I felt unable to have sex any more. He was saying that I had absolute responsibility for not having a baby and that if I made a mistake he would leave. There was no way of absolutely ensuring that I would not get pregnant without being sterilised and I didn't see why I should agree to that, a far more major operation, if he refused to have a vasectomy. I could not make love and he threatened me with a mistress unless I did.

This went on for some months and my periods became more and more heavy, more and more frequent; I think because I was so unhappy. In the end I went to my doctor and he sent me to a gynaecologist in London. He told me I had a hormonal imbalance, that hormones would help me. I asked if being on the pill would have the same effect and he said yes. I asked if he would prescribe the pill for me and he did so. I did not tell him about the depression they caused. I went back on the pill and began having sex again. I felt worn out and very down. My husband took a lover anyway.

Sarah

I've got a lot more

The pain, the twisted pain
that a pitiful man
can use
His failings,
His insecurities,
He uses to abuse
Someone too, who has
her failings
But knows her mind
and limitations.

He sticks the pins
He twists the knots
Sometimes I think
he could have the lot
Be rid of me
So he can't hurt anymore,
but then I know that
I've got a lot more

than he could dream of

A strength to go forward,
to sort my life out
with help from my friends
and the love from support.

Honesty is a non word
it is lost to this man
The little boy lost
Needs his mother and his torment
I get the shakes
my courage wanes
when the thought
of the pain comes
back again.
Where goes the strength
does it feed my own
problems?

Do I see him in me?
I have my own me
and to free it, is the key

Susan

We finished this chapter with Susan's poem, because it points to the hope that has helped so many women break free from violence.

CHAPTER TWO :
THE EFFECTS OF VIOLENCE
ON WOMEN AND CHILDREN

EFFECTS OF VIOLENCE ON CHILDREN

For this section, we made a list of all the ways that we thought our children had been affected by living in a violent home. We also remembered some of the feelings that we have had because of being brought up in that sort of atmosphere ourselves. Different children respond in different ways, but it is part of our struggle against violence to try to be aware of how our children are feeling. We want to help them become the happy people they deserve to be.

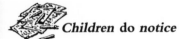

Children do notice

Children sense it at an early age — even as babies they would come down crying if we had an argument.

Even though I was only actually hit once, my son, who was only two, remembers it.

They seem alright, but things come out later. My son took some photos years after we had left, and they didn't come out. He said "You won't hit me will you Mum?"

My sons are quite grown-up now, but they still find it difficult if other women come to the house and talk to me about violence they are going through, because they just don't want to be reminded.

Confusion and guilt

Children feel they have to choose one parent.

They feel guilty for what has happened.

They find it hard to trust people.

I can remember fantasising that my parents would die — then felt really guilty — because I wasn't allowed to express my feelings. I didn't realise that it was OK to have bad thoughts.

It's worse if parents won't talk about it — I felt bitter because they wouldn't share what had happened — I felt that they had been hiding things from me.

Stunted emotional growth

Children make a shell around themselves.

They suppress their emotions — including their anger.

They have to grow up too quickly.

You've never experienced a situation where you can grow.

It's like a famine of the emotions.

You never learn to look at your emotions — or you deliberately hide them.

I used to smile so that people wouldn't know.

You avoid situations and relationships involving the emotions.

Lack of self confidence

They get very clingy.

Mine got very nervous.

I just had very low self esteem.

A feeling of powerlessness

Some children try to injure themselves — even as an adult you can get into a pattern where you are always ill, or getting into bad relationships.

I felt powerless to stop the arguing.

When you can't express how unhappy you are you learn not to bother — you feel rejected and bitter — it flattens you, it stops you trying.

I wasn't even aware of having any rights.

A feeling of "missing out"

It is as if the attention they should be getting is not there — I've caught myself doing it to my children — giving them attention on the surface but not really having anything to to give them — because I was missing out from what I needed.

They've got this feeling of being different.

They get embarrassed with other children about what's going on at home.

This feeling of having skeletons in the cupboard carries on into adulthood.

I used to fantasise about being a "normal" child.

The effect of violence on one family

I have three children, two girls and one boy, aged 7, 6 and 4. I've been on my own two years, so the eldest was just 5 a few weeks after I made the final break from my ex-husband, and she had just started school. I could see she was very withdrawn — she used to come out of school, happy, full of life, and would tell me about her day, but I always felt something deep was tearing her apart. I found it hard to ask her if it was because of her dad leaving. Then her Dad started coming round to see her and the other two. We both promised not to argue in front of them, which worked for a while, then the torment began.

I began to notice how she used to cry if I told her off. At night when she went to bed she would kiss me goodnight, and we would have a talk about the day so that she would know that I cared. After a while I would go to check on all three. The youngest would be asleep, but she would be sobbing. I used to get all upset — all the things I had gone through to pull myself together for their sake would all go down the drain. I would end up in floods of tears, but couldn't go into her room, because I felt that while I was like that I would upset her even more . . . Somehow I had to find a way of talking to her but didn't know how because at this time I was still very scared of losing my children because of what people and the professionals would think of the way I was looking after them. I went to her school to talk to her teacher but they said she was alright in school.

After a few nights of her crying and me trying to let her talk freely, I broke down yet again. I just fell on my bed after I tried to cuddle her and she had pushed me away, saying that she hated me. I felt a complete failure as her mother. I shut her door and just cried in sheer anger and frustration, asking "Why me?" I heard the door open. A small body jumped onto my bed next to me. We held each other tight and just cried together. I told her I missed her Dad and loved him very much, just as I loved her. I would like him back, but he didn't love me as he had another woman, and he couldn't live with us because he loved her more, and would never come back. I said I loved her, and somehow I would try to see if he would come to see her so that she wouldn't get upset. That night she slept with me. We had a good night's sleep and in the morning I tried to think of a way of talking my ex into coming to see the children. I spoke to my solicitor to arrange him seeing all three. Soon he was seeing them again. It started off every night, but after one of my children told him I had a boyfriend he got mad and started getting violent again. We arranged to meet at the

Sports Centre, but after a few weeks he gave up so I was back to square one.

She started to mess herself a few times. I said she must have an upset tummy, but I knew she hadn't — but it worked because very soon it stopped. Very soon everything blew over and we try to talk as much as we can about her Dad whenever the need crops up, because I feel with her she needs to know and understand why he isn't here.

The other day she asked "Why didn't Daddy hit me when he hit the other two?" I had a friend in the house at the time, and she was shocked even though she knew what went on. Even I don't know why, so that question stays unanswered. It's strange the way things have turned out. Although she was the one who never received any violence it hit her badly. I felt that I treated her badly, and different from the other two, but after great thought I realise that I treat her more like the eldest child — at times giving her a little more because she needs it.

She is at times insecure, like myself, and needs a little push in the right direction. I hope she pulls through and in later life becomes a confident adult and through past experiences becomes closer to me and her brother and sisters, realising that it is better to be without a father than go through what we all did. Though I hope in a few years their father will allow them to have contact because I realise that it's their right, not mine to do as I feel. I try now not to over protect them and do my best.

Out of the three, two of them did better out of the violent relationship right from the start, and now I can see the third has come to terms with it. It still hurts me to think there is no man around to give me a hand with bringing them up and sharing the joy of bringing them up like a stereotyped family as many of their friends. But so far I've not found a partner, mainly because I am scared of what they think. I don't go out very often now in fear of turning their world upside-down once again. It's taken a while to settle down like at the moment, though I feel my life's not what I want. But then seeing the happiness of my children makes me feel I can't gamble with what I've got. They have lost so much because of my past judgements — now I have to live for them.

On my own, I try to continue as a family, not isolating us from the community, just because we are one of the many products of a divorce brought on by violence. Their love is the best gift of all, and through them I've the strength to carry on, and hope all other children come through a broken marriage like them.

Elizabeth

THE EFECTS OF VIOLENCE ON WOMEN

Again, we started thinking about this topic by making a list — this time of all the effects violence had had on us as women.

It made us feel . . .

demoralised	resentful
degraded	insecure
afraid	unloved
introverted	unlovable
ugly	mistrustful
dreary	useless
worthless	inadequate
suicidal	confused
broken down	vulnerable
humiliated	depressed
switched off	aggressive
terrified	old
angry	hard
ashamed	emotionally and
guilty	physically drained

Some of us also . . .

Started to live up to the accusations that were made about us
Lost touch with ourselves, and what we wanted to do
Feared for our sanity
Began to think it was normal
Became agorophobic (afraid of open spaces)
Became violent ourselves
Lost touch with reality
Let ourselves be used sexually (some of us had no
choice in this anyway)
Gave in for a quiet life
Went outside for affection
Turned away from friends
Became physically ill
Became incontinent

Needed to inflict pain on ourselves — caused through totally
mixed emotions about the situation and through guilt about
how we allowed ourselves to be put into this position. (None
of us at the time realised how many other women were in
the same situation).

Rationalised the situation
Lied about what was happening to other people

After the relationship had finished we also . . .

Found it difficult to trust other men
Had difficulty in enjoying sex
Had a big need for love and affection
Found it hard to get back a willingness to go on with
life
Found it hard to find peace of mind — or to believe we
were normal

On the other hand, once we had left lots of positive things happened as well . . . see part 4 . . . especially our list of "gains after leaving a violent relationship . . . see p.89.

The effect of violence on one woman

It has made me feel very unsure of myself and very aware of men and frightened that it might happen again. Of course each time it happens it gets worse.

After a year I feel a bit mentally stronger, but still unsure of doing anything about my life.

I have now been on my own for nearly one year, but still find it hard at times to accept that things have come to this. I feel I have failed the children by taking them away from their dad and home.

At times I still wish someone was coming home later and that way I would get up and do things around the house. I tend to think sometimes oh! I'll leave it until tomorrow — no one will see it.

I am also frightened of being with male company on my own, because I feel they just want to use me because I'm on my own, and that I am longing for company. I feel as if I'm the only one in the world with my problems, and I hate making decisions about the children on my own.

While I was in the refuge I felt safe and I wasn't so alone, but at the same time I was longing for my own home.

Philippa

Effects of the violence — a group conversation

Not long after we started meeting as a group, we had this conversation about how the violence had affected us. Nothing will ever take away the seriousness of the effects of violence, but some us of, after nearly a year of working together now feel more able to rise above the effects that violence has had on our lives.

32

Louise. *I've lost some of my childhood memories. I've blanked off so much of what happened as an adult that I've lost them as well.*

Penny. Yes, people say "Penny, You've got a terrible memory".

L. *Even my eyesight and my hearing — they were perfect, but because I've had so many punches to the head, they're not as good as they were.*

Jenny. Sometimes I just sit and stare — it must be something in the past — it's like a cloud hanging over your head.

L. *A lot of people think I'm not normal — that I'm strange.*

J. Is it because you are very open?

L. *It could be. Once you have been humiliated so much there is nothing else to hide.*

Sylvia. I tend to shake — if I'm put in the slightest stressful situation I feel that the whole of me from head to foot is trembling — it doesn't have to be much that causes it, just something which brings it all up again.

P. *Yes. You know last week when we started talking about our situations, I felt all trembly inside — all jittery.*

S. I used to get the runs when I felt like that.

Amy. *Me too especially when I knew he was going to turn up after we had split up.*

L. It's awful isn't it.

A. *The other night (when I had to say something I didn't want to say) I felt awful.*

Diane. Though I think that's something that a lot of women feel even when they haven't suffered violence.

S. *I think that if you have been in a violent relationship and you have experienced what might happen — you know what you would have got if you stood up for yourself before, and somehow those feelings come back.*

P. If I'm wild or upset I shake something terrible — though I let it out and then I feel better.

J. *Do you get easily angry? I do about situations that I think children shouldn't be in — I probably get too angry. So angry that it sometimes gets in the way of being any help to them. I think that's because I went through so much as a child.*

S. Do you find that if you see something violent on TV that you feel withdrawn from all men — that happens to me. My bloke notices it. I can feel it in me — keeping myself to myself. I saw a programme where a woman was being treated badly the other night. I felt as if it was being done to me and I found myself looking at my boyfriend as if he was doing it!

Was it that film where a bloke was hitting a woman and she said sorry to him?

S. *Yes!*

D. People have talked about being in a relationship where they have almost lost their sanity, — have lost all sense of who they really are. Do you think that when you left the relationship, any of you were able to "find yourself" — and get back what you had lost?

J. *I think that some women don't find themselves for years and years and years.*

L. I'm not even sure that I know myself even now — I still get moments when I think that I'm mad — I get the same feelings out of the relationship as when I was in it.

J. *How long have you been out of it?*

L. 20 months.

J. *That's not long.*

L. But I don't think I'll ever be the person I was born to be. I feel that part of me has totally disappeared. It might not have been good, what I was meant for, but whatever it was has gone.

Elaine. *But people who knew you before must know that. My Dad used to say to me that I wasn't the same person that I had been before. I used to be a happy cheerful person. Now I can't think of anything to say let alone come out with a witty answer.*

L. I think that it's something that's lost. I think that half the time anyway.

A. *I agree with that —*

J. I don't agree — perhaps it's because it happened when I was a child — and yes I've made a few mistakes as an adult, but I just think that ok it's just taken me longer than it would have if it all hadn't happened. I'll get where I want to be.

Janet. *I think I'm getting nearer to the basic me — the me that I want to be. When you are in adolescence you begin to find out things about yourself and I lost that basic opportunity. My husband was 15 years older than me, and I jumped 15 years — I went in at his level — so I'd lost that bit in between. I don't think I can go back*

34

to my teens, but I feel that I'm finding what I wanted to then.

L.   Isn't it an awful tragedy!

Janet.   *But I'm trying not to let my conditioning stop me finding myself. I never loved the man — it was how I was conditioned, and what I thought was right, and what I thought was wrong.*

That's how I feel. I know I couldn't do it on my own. I just felt that I wanted to die. It's taken me three years — not that it's ever right — it's an ongoing growing struggle. Sometimes you struggle more than you grow but I do feel that there is growth.

I'm coming out with so many hangups — in a stressful situation I just get the jitters — I get the runs and I feel that I have to get out. But perhaps in ten years time I will be able to cope with things like that. I'm only 27 — and I think that I can live with the fact that it will take time.

Still three years on I go to counselling.

L.   But lots of women don't have counselling — they don't have that professional help to bring them back so . . . they are lost . . . perhaps they never find out about themselves and how they want to be.

Janet.   *I think three years is early days — I don't say to myself — "come on it's three years now you should be over it". It's part of my life — these experiences. I find it very hard to let go.*

When I find myself shaking I get angry with myself — I have to tell myself that it's not really my fault that I'm feeling like that. I get angry that I've allowed myself to be trampled on. I think it's probably certain processes that we really have to go through — though sometimes I think we could do without it — all this having to go back and trace back, churning all these things over in your brain.

D.   Do people feel that they have actually gained anything from what they have been through and from having to struggle with it?

Amy.   *You get to know your mistakes — and to think about things better.*

Caroline.   You feel stronger — I won't let myself be trampled on again — and I feel that I'm a bit aggressive because I don't want that to happen — and maybe I'll lose out on relationships — because I'll be suspicious.

Penny.   *I tend to fight back first before they put me down. But I've learned now to keep my mouth shut a bit more.*

IF IT'S SO BAD WHY DO WOMEN PUT UP WITH IT?

One of the most hurtful things that people can say about women trying to escape from violence is "It can't have been that bad or she wouldn't have put up with it for so long" or "I can't understand why she went back to him — some women just can't make up their minds."

Most women in our group have left their violent partners for good. The decision to leave was not easy for any of us though, and some of us did leave and go back a few times. We also know women from our local Women's Aid refuge who have gone back to violent relationships. We think it is important to understand some of the reasons why it is so hard to make the initial break — and then stick to it.

The first thing to remember it that it takes a tremendous amount of courage to leave in the first place.

If you look back through this chapter at the way that violence makes women feel you will find words like

humiliated, demoralised, ashamed, useless

Not a state of mind that most people would choose to embark on a new life with.

The question should not be

"Why do women put up with it for so long?"

but

"Where do women get the courage from to start a new life when they're feeling like that?"

What about women who keep going back?

If it takes courage to leave a violent relationship, it also takes courage to stick with this decision. Some of the factors which have made this hard for us and for other women that we know are:

- Having to wait for months in an overcrowded refuge before being rehoused.
- The law gives women very little protection if they decide to go back to their own house with a legal injunction to keep the man out.
- The housing we have been offered is often not very good.
- It can take great courage to cope with life as a single parent — coping

with loneliness, lack of money, poor public transport, lack of childcare and work opportunities.

- The children often miss their father.
- Women often still love their partners, and hope they will change.
- We have been brought up to believe that success or failure for us as women hinges on whether we are successful in our relationships with men.

In spite of the fact that it is so hard to leave — and to stay away — the fact is that many perfectly ordinary women like ourselves *do* find the courage to do this.

There have been many things which have been positive along the way — many of which we hope to explain later in this book.

— e.g. refuges may be overcrowded but they also offer a lot of support *(See chapter 6)*
— some of us have found other ways of feeling accepted and valued, e.g. through our friendship with other women, or by working through Women's Aid to support other women.

For any woman reading this book who wants to leave the violence but feels she isn't strong enough yet, we would like to say two things:

1. Don't blame yourself for not being ready yet.

and

2. Try to find someone to give you support.
(Chapters 5 and 6 will give you some ideas of organisations you can go to — or try to find a woman friend who will back you up.)

CHAPTER 3:
SEXUAL ABUSE OF CHILDREN

Suburbs

> We walked along the road,
> Pleasant suburbia it seemed;
> Long lines of houses in red brick,
> Lace curtains hanging, straight and white
> A respectable district. At one we stopped.
> The blue front door, shining and smart
> Opened, children tumbled out
> And ran off down the street.
> Through open windows, a couple,
> Man and woman, stripped wallpaper.
> A radio blared and died away. Then
> The wordless rhythm of conversation,
> The woman laughed and left the room.
> The one with me moved towards me,
> "In that house", she said, "My father raped me,
> My mother cut her wrists before my eyes."

Sarah

This has been the hardest chapter in the book to discuss and write. Some women in the group have been in relationships where their own children have been abused, others have been sexually abused themselves as children. Some women have talked about their experience for the very first time. Sharing what has happened to them has taken great courage.

Although Caroline cannot remember actual sexual abuse, some of the feelings she expresses might well strike a chord with women who have. It reminds us that there is something basically damaging to a child whem the adult who cares for them expects them to fulfil adult rather than child-like roles. (Which of course is one of the things which is happening when children are sexually abused).

Looking back nearly a third of my life later, I realise that my problems really began to start when my Uncle took me to the local jewellery shop and asked me what ring I would like. I was five at the time, and, looking back, it was like a ring of ownership — somehow I belonged to him. It was only a few years ago that I could look at him in a critical light; this man who was everything to my young life — I really felt in debt to him. I felt I was totally responsible for him and his happiness. It was far too close a relationship, and even now I am a mother with children of my own I am still working my way through it.

I think I was like a wife to him because he never married and he moulded and shaped me the way he wanted. It was never what he said, but the silences, and he always made me feel guilty. My school friends, I remember, were very envious, especially when he would take us all to the pictures and buy us all lots of sweets, but this in itself would make me feel very alien to my friends. Gradually I was becoming more and more isolated, I think because it was such an unusual relationship. He lived in the same house with my grandparents, who were in charge of bringing me up, and yet I can only remember being with him. I used to always feel so guilty — in fact it was not until he died that I felt free, and even now I am still working out where I am in it all.

A good father

He was a good father.
Everyone said so;
Coping so well
With his dying wife
The children always quiet
And well-behaved.
His daughter he loved,
Everybody said so;
The way he taught her,
They did everything
Together.

At night naked
In her bedroom
He taught her
Other secret things
Sometimes he thought
She might be beautiful
But that was not the thing to tell her.
He was a good father
He'd save her from the sin
Of pride.

At school she wrote obliquely
Violent metaphors of men
Of silent mutilations
Red messages of pain.
The teachers could not
Understand it —
She had a good father.
Everyone knew him —
Returned her work.
"Please write again.
Unsuitable."

Sarah

Jenny talks about the effect on her adult life of being sexually abused as a child, and of her struggle to come to terms with it.

Breaking through

I was sexually abused from the age of 5 to 14 — for seven years by my father, and for two years by the man my mother chose to replace him. I left home and school just before I was 15 to get the hell out of it.

It seemed to me for the next 10 years that I was leading a normal life. I trained as a nurse, I then got married and had children. Both my mother and my grandmother were very ill over quite a long period of time, which meant I looked after two small children and also travelled regularly long distances to be with them until they died.

I became involved, (as if this wasn't enough), with every caring organisation you could imagine — e.g. Age Concern, Social Services, the local hospice — in fact, anything that constantly reminded me that people were much worse off than myself. What was really happening was that all of this enabled me to numb any real feelings I might have had about myself, and blocked off all I didn't want to think about. It also reinforced the role of caring for others — doing what others would wish of me — and there must have been something not quite right about that. This pattern continued until I was in my early thirties, although I had by then made one step towards questioning what I was doing, by becoming a single parent. This was at least a conscious decision after years of making the fatal mistake of thinking "But I must have a partner — I have to prove to the world I can make this work. What will the world think of me if I don't make it work?" What was so ridiculous was that I didn't even know myself or even like myself during this time. Although I moved around a bit in relationships after my marriage had broken up, I could not allow the trust and growth of a relationship — and to think that I even took on the responsiblity of forming relationships!

This leads me on to how I feel now after experiencing two years of emotional hard work on my part and lots of loving support from my friends. I look back now and think I must have been making a subconscious effort before all this hard work began, to build a network of loving caring friends around me as a safety net to give myself the courage to look at myself honestly.

It took me ten weeks to go through my "breakthrough" — I prefer to call it that more than the more conventional breakdown, it has a more positive feel to it. There I was having to accept that nearly half my life I had been used, abused, denied, violated, rejected — in fact that I had had to go through every feeling of being worthless, unwanted and unloved. It's not surprising that I fought on the edge of wondering whether I could even continue my life with such a realisation. I couldn't believe at times that it could ever get better. I had to be taught like a child to express my anger, sadness, loneliness and to actually feel within my rights to do this. (I was so worried all the time about the effect on other people — after all I was the one who people would say about "Doesn't she cope well", "Isn't she a good mother? A good listener?" If only they knew that all the time I was keeping a lid on a can of worms.

Reluctantly I started counselling. It was hard for me as of course I was such a good coper — I used to think "I don't want to waste anyone's time. Other people are far worse off than me". The counsellor continued for a year and, with constant and reliable support from my friends, I managed to really face up to what had happened to me as a child and to deal with it.

When I flung total negativity at my friends they always believed in me first and foremost. I'm sure I was trying to get them to admit I wasn't worth it — at least that way, I could have forgotten all about it and retreated into a person who was only half alive. I wouldn't have had to believe in myself, which was of course what I had been experiencing up until that point.

Two years on from that time, and I feel strong, able to cry, feel angry, and realise it is safe to have these emotions. The most important thing for me is that I have choice, and that the decisions I make are about what's right for me. I am learning, although this isn't easy, to love myself and to accept myself. I try not to analyse all the time now, and I use my intuition as much as possible — but you do have to feel very positive about yourself to do this.

I was raped last summer, and, terrible though the experience was, it did prove to me that I was able to use, and put into practice, everything that I had learned during my breakthrough. This time I didn't deny myself the feelings that I needed to work through what had happened to me, nor did I blame myself for it as I might have done in the past.

Violation of any form, forced on women and children by men, leaves a scar. It cannot be removed. Without the care and love surrounding me when I most needed it I could never have come to terms with my earlier life. But what a shame my life only began in my early thirties and not before. Many many other women's lives have not even begun.

Jenny

WHO DOES INCEST* AFFECT?

- *Many more children than the statistics are ever likely to show — as the recent Childwatch campaign has shown, once you make it possible for children to talk about what is happening more and more cases come to light.*

- *Children from babyhood right through to adolescence — it is not, as many people believe, a problem which only affects teenagers.*

- *Children in all classes of society.*

- *Girls more than boys — we have seen estimates that 9 out of 10 incest cases are abuse by an adult male of a girl in his "care".*

- *Adult women who were abused as children — who carry a burden, often in complete silence — throughout their life.*

HOW DOES INCEST AFFECT CHILDREN AND ADULT WOMEN?

Some of the effects talked about in our group have been —

- Feelings of guilt and shame and extreme confusion.

- Isolation — because either they did not talk about what had happened, or were not believed.

- Hatred of oneself — feeling unworthy and "dirty".

- Total loss of trust towards any male.

- Possible feelings of betrayal by the mother. (Even when she does not know what is going on, the child will look to her for protection.)

- Allowing people to use you because of your lack of self worth.

- Feeling responsible throughout life for everyone else's problems. Feeling that we owe people something — e.g. that we should sleep with men if they take us out for the evening.

We have talked mostly of the emotional effects here, but for children there are obvious **physical** *effects — internal injury, infections, venereal disease, pregnancy, and now, the danger of AIDS. In addition, some men use other forms of physical violence when they abuse children sexually.*

---

* We are using a wider definition of incest than the legal one, which relates to actual sexual intercourse. We include in our definition any sexual abuse by an adult of a child in their care. Information in this chapter from Sarah Nelson, *Incest Fact and Myth*, a very useful book.

Two women in the group have written about what happened to them and the effect it had.

My childhood was a bit of a turmoil at any rate, and some of it is difficult to place and understand. Mainly because I was too young to know what was going on around me.

As I grew older however, things became clearer. My mother was living with a bloke, and they were having some shape of a relationship which I still can't understand. This bloke used to touch me up. At first he'd be playing with me, tickling me and such, then the tickles would get to more intimate places. I used to complain, to ask my mother to stop, as I didn't like it. She would tell me to stop inventing things. When I was about 13 and until I was nearly 16, my mother would take me to his room every Sunday morning and he'd play/tickle me in his bed. He used to get a hard-on which he used to hold me up close to. I hated every minute of it. Just before my 16th birthday I ran away from home — the police brought me back a week later. My step-father/uncle was in tears locked away in his room. My mother told me how he had said that he loved me and wanted me. My mother asked me to go along with it. She said "Just sleep with him, you don't have to marry him. I have a lot of money invested in his name, just do it until I can get my money back."

A month after my 16th birthday I left home, never to return. My mother and him are still together today, 14 years later.

Sylvia

Sarah's story

Sometimes I think that the worst aspect of my father's violence was how grateful I felt to him. My mother abandoned me in the hospital when I was born and it was my father who came to get me. My mother developed cancer because of an accident after my birth and found it difficult to deal with me — so a great part of my pre-school years I spent either alone or with my father. He had great control of my life from early on, began teaching me to read when I was two, and after that giving me weekly tests. We lived in the country then and we moved when I was seven. Things changed then; my mother's cancer got worse, she spent most of the time in bed. I don't know how it began, but my father started coming naked into my bedroom at night. He became very aroused, but did not penetrate me. The worst shame is that I know I was aroused by him. I knew that I couldn't tell anyone about all this. I remember feeling pleased because people thought I was happy — I was always smiling. I felt glad that they could not see what was underneath. Yet despite the smiles I was truanting regularly, getting more and more asthma. When I was ten I tried to cut my wrists. My mother started taking overdoses in my teens. In my late teens I did too — all the anger I felt I directed against myself. When I started my periods, my father stopped coming to my room. I felt glad and rejected.

I stopped being successful at school at the same time — I'm not sure whether this was because I felt rejected and unloved by him, or because it was a way of being angry at him. Without success he was no longer interested in me and I left school at 15 because he refused to buy my school uniform — I "didn't deserve it".

He still tries to control what I wear and do; this has always (until recently) stopped me going on to study, because it would please him. Even though I must have been desirable to him he has always told me that I am ugly, would tell me that I wouldn't get married. When he has promised love and support, he would let me down. I accepted this pattern and married a man who continued to tease in this way.

COMMON MYTHS ABOUT INCEST

The myth of childhood fantasy

Because the truth about sexual abuse of children is so difficult to face up to, many people prefer to believe that it is all in the mind of the child. They are encouraged in this by a long tradition in psychiatry which prefers to give the benefit of the doubt to male abusers rather than to children.*

* The "Oedipus complex, Freud's famous theory which talks of the way that children have sexual desires for their parents arose from the fact that many of his women patients were telling him about their childhood experiences of incest. At first he believed them, but then later changed his mind. So . . . because he and the medical establishment of the time couldn't cope with the tought of respectable men abusing their daughters, many thousands of children have since been disbelieved. (For a fuller discussion of this see Sarah Nelson, *Incest Fact and Myth*.)

Those of us who have struggled to face up to what has happened, know that this myth of childhood fantasy about incest simply IS NOT TRUE. Our view is confirmed by many people working with children who are suffering abuse.

The fantasy theory is very powerful and very damaging however.

- It allows men — who are the main culprits — to carry on abusing the children in their care.
- It means that many children still aren't believed.
- It makes adults less ready to "pick up the signs" often given by abused children that something is badly wrong.

One of the ways that children deal with sexual abuse is by "blocking off" what has happened to them. This is something that all women in our group who are incest survivors have done. Because of this it is hard enough anyway to actually face and work through what has happened.

Sarah has written about how this natural tendency to "block out" incest experiences was increased in her case by the way that she *herself* has accepted this fantasy theory.

I protected my father from bearing the responsibility of incest. The only way I could do this was by blocking off that part of my childhood even from myself, and so that was what I did — I forgot. I was 37 when I finally managed to break through all that protection. When I was 25 I spent a year in a therapeutic community, but I spent that time working through my mother's abuse of me.

In the last five years since my husband left, I can see now that there were times when I was trying to get to the point of remembering. The first time I went to a local Catholic priest, whom I trusted more than any man I knew. I went after a year of being a single parent, thinking that I needed to work out unresolved feelings about my husband. It quickly became obvious to me that there were even more important things that I had to learn, but I could not think what they were. I looked at the situation: I trusted this priest more than any other man, and I trusted myself, so I felt that I would not get into the same sexual situation with this man as I had with others before. (I had many years before had a sexual relationship with a priest and a doctor — men, who like my father, should have been trustworthy and weren't.) Then I remember having this overwhelming sensation of jumping off into an abyss — of not knowing where I was going or what

46

would happen, but that it was so important — of absolute importance. I just trusted that it would be alright. I don't remember the sessions very clearly — it was very scrambled, but I had the sensation of getting really close to something, of walking my way through darkness. Then one day the priest phoned. He told me never to come to the presbytery again. I thought for weeks that I would just die with the pain — I had felt so close to what I needed to know. I remember thinking that perhaps I should have begged him to let me go on. Slowly I recovered from that, knowing that I still needed to work things out. Two years later I went to Marriage Guidance, but there I didn't develop the trust I needed with the counsellor to begin. Even though she was a woman, I think that that particular counsellor found it very difficult to look at areas I was edging towards unconsciously.

It was not until I went on an all-woman Second Chance to Learn course to try and find out why I could not learn in a conventional way that I felt safe enough to take that leap again. It was there, as we looked back on our earliest learning experiences that I began to have flashbacks of my father. At first these were like short snatches from a video in my head. I thought I was going mad. I thought "How could this have really happened to someone and then been forgotten? It was impossible". At last I told my tutor and I don't think that she will ever know what she did for me that day. She held me and believed me and it was trusting her and knowing that she trusted me that allowed me to start this journey.

Even so, I still had all these awful doubts in myself, that really I was pretending. It was that that made me ring the therapist I had in the community, someone I loved as a mother, to see what she felt about these flash-backs. It was her response that allowed me to begin to believe myself.

The "she asked for it myth"

It is men who are guilty of sexually abusing children — encouraged, we feel, by the centuries old tradition of male dominance. If men have sexual "rights" over women then tragically these are exercised all too often over children.

Some people however actually feel that it is children who seduce their fathers, grandfathers, uncles etc. WE FIND THIS IS TOTALLY UNACCEPTABLE.

● *It ignores the feelings of revulsion that many children feel, not to mention the actual physical damage which they can experience.*

- *It misinterprets the natural physical affection which children have the RIGHT to show to those who care for them, and sees it from an adult's rather than a child's perspective.*

- *It puts the responsibility on the child rather than the adult. Even if some children do experience sexual desire for the adults who care for them, then it is the adult's responsibility to protect them from the confusion and harm that a sexual relationship with an adult involves for a child.*

Sarah expresses the feelings of guilt that she felt as an adult coming to terms with incest. As with the fantasy myth, the "She asked for it" myth can only add to the damage caused to children and women.

On two occasions when I was younger I got myself into sexual relationships with men who should have been unassailable. The first time,when I was 18 I became very fond of a priest in the parish that I was living in at the time. I was very attracted to him, and yet, when I discovered that he was attracted to me, I felt terrible. This was not what I wanted and I felt ashamed and guilty that he did. Yet I felt that if he wanted my body it was his right to have it, and we became lovers. He made me promise never to tell anyone.

A year or so later in another part of the country, I developed a similar relationship with my G.P. and the same thing happened again. I finished up feeling anger, humiliation and disgust at myself. I thought that there must be something truly wicked about me if I could seduce such men. They, like my father, a teacher, were "good men" — their professions told me that. I was sickened by myself, by the secrets that I locked up inside myself. I was too ashamed to tell anyone even when I was in therapeutic community, and it wasn't until years and years after that that I ever told anyone.

Now I know that I was only repeating what had happened between my father and I when I was a child. I also know that the relationship I really wanted with these men was the relationship I really wanted with my father; affection and love that was safe.

The "Blaming the Mother" myth

This section perhaps caused more heated discussion and pain even than the rest of this chapter. Basically the problem is that we are tired of women being blamed for male violence and yet some women in the group have a deep and lasting anger against their mothers for either "allowing" them to be abused as children by not noticing what was going on, or in one woman's case by actively encouraging what was happening.

This negative feeling towards mothers whose daughters are sexually abused by men in the home is certainly echoed by many books written on the subject,where the mother is often referred to as the "passive partner" in the abuse. WE FEEL THAT IN GENERAL THIS IS VERY UNFAIR.

In the end we felt that we needed to say two things which at first seem to contradict one another.

The first is a message for women who are trying to cope with the sexual abuse they received as children — and also to girls and young women who are doing this.

> "If you feel angry with your mother as well as your father, then this is something that everyone in your situation is likely to feel. It is not something to feel guilty about, but which you have a right to express and work through — often with the help of someone who really understands what you are going through. You may not feel that you even want to look into reasons which explain or excuse your mother's behaviour. You may well have gone through life, like some of us have, feeling responsible for everyone else — it is YOU who needs looking after and deserves attention."

The second is a message for mothers of girls who might be at risk, and for those who are in a position to help them.

> "OF COURSE women need to be on the watch for signs that their children are being sexually abused. This takes a lot of courage however. Mothers are much more likely to be able to protect their children if they are given the SUPPORT they need rather than being pushed down even further by having all the BLAME for the situation heaped on them. IN THE END WE MUST REMEMBER THAT IT IS USUALLY *MEN* WHO ABUSE GIRLS.

As part of giving support to women in this situation some important points need to be remembered:

● Men who abuse children are also often violent to their wives or partners, and many women may be genuinely too frightened to do anything about the abuse of their children.

● Even when sexual abusers are not actually physically violent to their partners they are llikely to have a strong sense of their "rights" in sexual matters, which are not going to lead to happy sexual relationships. ALL OF US try to block out the reality of incest. It is even more likely that a woman living in such a relationship is going to be "blocking out" her sexual feelings, and will be even less open to the "signals" that her daughter may be giving out that something is wrong.

In the end we don't think our two messages do contradict each other. On the one had we are saying "Incest victims have a right to feel angry with their mothers" (and their fathers of course); *and on the other hand we are saying* "Women need understanding, support and resources in order to protect their children from abuse."

ABUSE OF POWER — THE ROOT CAUSE OF INCEST

When we discuss the causes of male violence to women in part 2 of this book, we shall discuss how each individual is affected by the way society expects them to behave. We believe strongly that individual men are encouraged in their violence by the way society expects them to be dominant — and we believe that this applies to sexual abuse of children as well.

There is something additional when we are talking about abuse of children however. If women are often not respected and given equal treatment then this is probably even more true for children — boys and girls — in their relationship with adults. One of the things we can do to help children to protect themselves from abuse is to a) break the taboo on talking about sexual abuse, and b) give them a strong sense of their own rights. At first talking about children's rights can seem a very strange idea, as we are so used to the idea that children should "do as they are told". In this chapter however we have seen the consequences of not taking children's rights seriously. In chapter 9 we shall be looking more closely at the whole issue of how we should bring up our children in a society where male violence is such a problem.

DANGER SIGNS

We would like to finish this chapter with a list of signs which might indicate that a child is being sexually assaulted. We have taken this list from information in SEXUAL VIOLENCE The Reality for Women, *the London Rape Crisis Centre.*

— Sudden change in attitude towards a particular man or men

— Expressing affection in overtly sexual ways

— Sleep problems

— Sudden behaviour changes

— Any indications that she is unhappy or disturbed

Every child will react in her own way, and perhaps the most useful thing which adults can do is to contstantly be aware that sexual assault of children is possible — and to ensure that they are given the time and respect from adults which will enable them to talk about it if they need to. Believing children, and taking their fears seriously is crucial.

CHAPTER 4:
HELPFUL AND UNHELPFUL EXPLANATIONS
FOR MALE VIOLENCE

"AS IF WE DIDN'T HAVE ENOUGH TO COPE WITH! —
EXPLANATIONS WHICH BLAME THE WOMAN

In the first part of this book, we have shown what male violence has meant to us and to countless other women and girls. So . . . what causes it? We started thinking about this by making a long list of all the explanations that we had heard. We didn't agree with all of them — in fact we didn't agree with most of them — but we need to know what other people might be thinking!

The thing which struck us most was that most of the explanations we came up with, BLAMED THE WOMAN! Common sense told us that this wasn't fair — it's bad enough being at the receiving end of violence without being blamed for it as well! Here are some of the women-blaming explanations we have heard:

> *Drink*　　　　*Expressing Jealousy*　　　　*Bad Housekeeping*
> *Spending too much time out of the family or with friends*
> *Pre-menstrual tension and having a period*
> *Going away from traditional roles, e.g.*
> *being too independent and "answering back"*
> *Being too timid*　　　*Having bad habits*　　　*Dropping things*
> *Touching "his" belongings*　　　　*Sitting in "his" chair*
> *Making him give up his hobbies, e.g. football*
> *Witholding or demanding sex — "the headache syndrome"*
> *Not being able to have children — or becoming pregnant*
> *Giving too much attention to the children*
> *Not controlling the children*　　　*Keeping an untidy home*
> *Protecting the children from the abuse*

Explanations that blame the woman go on and on. Sometimes they are the excuses given by the man for his behaviour, sometimes they are explanations given by perfectly "well-meaning" people — doctors, social workers, friends, family etc.

We are not printing all these woman-blaming explanations to make women feel even more guilty — just to show what we are up against! We have all gone through times when we blame ourselves. Not only does this not make sense, it can also stop us having the confidence to challenge the violence and get on with the job of rebuilding our lives.

In fact LEARNING NOT TO BLAME HERSELF IS THE FIRST IMPORTANT STEP for a woman in learning to deal with male violence.

*Let's think back to Elizabeth's story in Chapter 1 — there she was, black and blue, struggling to look after a new born baby and two toddlers and her "friend" arrived and started blaming **her** for not keeping a spotlessly clean house! Another extract from Elizabeth's story shows what she had to do to live a life where she couldn't be blamed for anything.*

I used to wake at 5 am because of the slimming tablets. I used to shower, dress myself, put some washing in the machine or hang out if I had washed the night before. Most nights I would have hoovered and polished, but I would start again in the morning. The girls would wake up, I would pop the youngest in the bath because she always smelt of stale urine. The eldest sometimes got in with her, but I used to give them a bath before bed. I would then give them breakfast. By this time it was getting on for 7.30, so they would be clean and pretty for when their Dad came home from the night shift. By the time my ex-husband went to bed the youngest would go back to sleep and sometimes the eldest. I would go back to bed, make love to my husband, then shower, wake up my daughter, give them a drink. If it was hot we used to go for nice walks with a packed lunch. I would return home, do all of my ironing straight from the dry washing on the line, prepare tea, wake up my ex, make love again, cook the evening meal, see him off to work, clean the kids in the bath, jump in with them, put them in bed, clean the house. Everything was repeated over and over again, because I was scared he would pick fault. I enjoyed doing it while I had the energy, but when I felt tired, that's when my nightmares began.

Most of us aren't prepared to lead such a "blameless" life, and, even if she had wanted to, Elizabeth just could not keep it up!

So . . . if we refuse to blame ourselves — who or what is to blame?

ARE PROBLEM FAMILIES TO BLAME?

Many people blame male violence towards women on something called the *"Cycle of violence theory".* Basically, what this theory states is that violence is passed down from one generation tot he next. This is not only taken to mean that the man learns to be violent because of a violent childhood, but that the woman also learns from her childhood to tolerate violence, to provoke it, or — most offensive of all — to grow to need it. So . . . the theory does not actually blame the woman, but it implies that it is because she does not know any better that the violence happens.

People often talk about this theory as if it was scientific fact. It has never been proved however, and indeed some people have strongly criticised the research on which the theory is based.★

Believing that one's family background is the MAIN CAUSE of violence in a relationship can have several bad effects . . .

- *People feel they cannot get out of the cycle*
- *There is a feeling that women in a violent situation don't know any different*
- *This can then become an excuse which prevents some professionals from helping women in violent situations, or directing them to do something positive for themselves*
- *People can be labelled. The fear of being labelled can stop some women admitting to the violence in their lives (e.g. some of us were afraid of admitting we had been in a refuge. One woman was afraid people wouldn't trust her with their children because she had been violated as a child).*

Women feel they cannot get out of the cycle

The problem with this theory is that at first sight it *seems* to make sense. Within our group, for example, several of us *have* suffered violence as children, and *have also entered violent relationships.* Because of this, it has been tempting to look no further than the cycle of violence theory in explaining the violence we have received.

We feel however that looking at our childhood background does not get to the heart of what is going on. It may explain a bit about *why we find*

★ *The Existing Research into Battered Women.* Elizabeth Wilson 1976, Women's Aid Federation.

ourselves in violent situations — some of us feel for example that having difficult backgrounds might have sapped our confidence so much that we have accepted behaviour from men that was a lot less than we deserved. What it doesn't explain is *why the violence began in the first place — WHY there were so many violent families when we were children, and why there are so many today.* To explain that we will have to go beyond the individual, and their family, and look at the society which each person and family belongs to.

The last thing we would like to say about the Cycle of Violence theory, is that those of us who did have a difficult upbringing do not see it in any way as a TRAP. Within ourselves, and with the support of others, we have found the strength to break away from the supposed pattern of violence. We are sure that many other women and children can do the same.

WHAT ABOUT POVERTY AND POOR LIVING CONDITIONS? OR DRINK?

Going back to our original list of explanations we had heard for male violence, we came up with reasons like:

> *unemployment*
> *poor living conditions*
> *lack of money*

At least these reasons go beyond the individual and make some link between individual violence and the conditions in which many people have to live.

There are still some problems with such "social explanations" however.

● If violence is *caused* by unemployment why are so many men in work violent to their wives and daughters?

● If violence is *caused* by poverty and overcrowding why do some men in very high status well paid jobs beat their partners?

Poor social conditions, like a violent upbringing (and drinking too much),probably add to the pressures on people, but in themselves they do not offer a complete explanation.

MACHO MAN — THE ROOT OF THE PROBLEM

So far in all this, we have not said much about the *man's* role in violence towards women. It is significant that when we made our original list of explanations, the number of items which even mentioned the man were MUCH fewer than those mentioning the woman! WHY AREN'T PEOPLE WONDERING WHAT CAUSES *MEN* TO BE SO VIOLENT INSTEAD OF LOOKING FOR WHAT IT IS IN *WOMEN* THAT PROVOKES THE VIOLENCE?

From our discussions a few possible thoughts on this have emerged.

- Because it is *women* who suffer from the violence, it is they who usually seek help from various agencies. From this it is a short (if not very intelligent) step for professionals to think that it is *women* who are at the root of the problem. This has happened several times to women in our group, and has also been described by writers on domestic violence, like R. Emerson and Russell Dobash and Elizabeth Wilson.* Elizabeth Wilson, for example, writes of the psychiatrist Dr J Gayford's insulting study which looked at male violence to women in terms of the sort of women affected — "Tortured Tina", "Go-go Gloria" etc.

- Another clue as to why so little attention is paid to the *men* who are actually *guilty* of the violence lies in the way that women are held responsible for *so much* that goes wrong with the family — vandalism, and delinquency is blamed on mothers who work; and of course, however many other adults are in the household, it is women who are often blamed if the house is dirty or the meals not on time. Even within our group we have found ourselves directing our anger at ourselves and — in the case of childhood sexual abuse — at our mothers, instead of at the men who are responsible for the abuse. It may seem an obvious point, but within a woman-blaming society, it needs to be said — MEN ARE RESPONSIBLE FOR MALE VIOLENCE.

So if men are the problem — what causes them to be violent? After a lot of discussion we have come to the conclusion that, at the root of the problem, is the way that all men and all women have traditionally been expected to behave towards each other — with men being expected to be dominant (and not to be "weak" and express their feelings) and for women to be submissive, attractive and domesticated.

* Elizabeth Wilson, *What is to be done about Violence Against Women*, Penguin
  R. Emerson and Russell Dobash, *Violence against Wives*, Open Books, Ch. 10,

We feel that it is important to see this link between violence and "normal" male/female relationships, so that we can question and challenge the countless subtle ways in which men are actually *encouraged* to be violent towards women.

We would like to spend the rest of the chapter discussing this.

1. THE HUSBAND!

You should

... be tough - like Rambo

WHAT MAKES MEN 'MACHO'?

So . . . where and how do people learn that men are supposed to be the "tough" "dominant" "macho" figure and women the "submissive" "soft" "attractive" "good" housewife and mother.

In our experience we have found that:

● *Men dislike to be proven to be in the wrong.*

● *Men dislike to be seen in a "feminine" situation, like changing nappies, especially in front of relatives or friends.*

● *Men find it hard to express their emotional feelings within a relationship.*

We have found things like these make men uptight and defensive of their male roles.

Here are some of the ways that pressure is put on men and women to behave in stereotyped ways.

Sign here please

Children's toys

... hold the purse-strings

Boys' toys are weapons of power — guns, action man, super heroes, tool kits . . .
Girls' toys are soft, pretty and encourage mothering — dolls, prams, tea sets, home equipment, make up mannequins.

Traditional sayings don't help

— *Who wears the trousers?*
— *You've got him/her trained all right*
— *The strong silent type*
— *The perfect wife is a chef in the kitchen a lady in the sitting room and a whore in bed*
— *She has got him twisted round her little finger*
— *He's got her right under his thumb*
— *Big boys don't cry*
— *Only sissies play with dolls*

You should NOT

... cry or show your emotions

Family and friends

Family and friends put pressure on men and women to behave in particular ways. How many mother in law jokes do you know — a prime example of the message "it's OK to ricicule women". Also, perhaps, a symptom of many men's unease in dealing with women who have any kind of power or influence over them.

Another example of men being pressurised into confirming to the stereotype is a typical situation of a man being with his mates at the pub. Man says he wants to go home early to help woman bath baby. The comments from his mates may include "What are you a man or a wimp", "But that's her job isn't it". By the time he gets home, he is feeling pressure and possibly BANG.

The structure of the schooling system

This can still be seen to reinforce male dominance and female submission, although things are improving.

In some schools boys and girls still file up in separate lines, the girls always going into school first.

The school's curriculum is still pretty sexist. Girls have less opportunity to do so-called "boy's" subjects.

There are more female first school and nursery teachers than males. Young children learn that children are looked after by women. Perhaps this may be because teachers for young children have less "status" attached to their job. Therefore men go for jobs with older children which have more "status" and higher pay.

And how does the media portray women?

One of the images is the "competent" housewife who has the meal on the table, the children sitting down to eat, all smiling when the man returns home from work in the evening — all with the help of an OXO cube! How real is this when nine times out of ten, a child wants to go to the loo, a glass of water gets knocked over, and in the meantime the gravy goes lumpy! Then the man comes in and says "Why can't you make gravy like in the adverts!!!" Well . . . we will leave the rest to your imagination!

Another image that the media imposes on women makes us feel that our body in its natural state is not good enough for our partners. Hence we are encouraged to wear cosmetics, to watch what we eat, remove our body hair and hide our periods. Within our group we have experienced men finding us dirty when we menstruate, to the extent that some of us have been hit for it.

At the extreme end of this view of women we come to pornography, ranging from page three to sex-shops selling "sexy" gear for us to wear to please our men. Many women, given a real choice, don't like this.

2. THE WIFE !

Your wife should

... be attractive

What about the law in all of this?

It is now actually against the law for a man to beat his wife — just as it would be against the law for him to beat anyone else. The Police still generally see this as "only domestic" however, and courts give ridiculously low sentences for assaults against wives. For example, in a recent survey, 59 women were asked to describe what had happened when they called the police out after the worst assault on them. Only 10 charges were made, and NO men were put in prison. This was in spite of the fact that 25 of the women had experienced life threatening assaults — e.g. involving attempted strangulation or drowning, or resulting in hospitalisation. (The other 34 had experienced severe bruising, black eyes etc.)*

This can be seen as part of a legal tradition in this country which actually recognises men's rights to have control over their wives. As late as 1915 a London magistrate gave his opinion that "the husband of a nagging wife . . . could beat her at home provided the stick he used was no thicker than a man's thumb". Nowadays IT IS STILL LEGAL FOR A MAN TO RAPE HIS WIFE.

The message given to men by the legal system is clear — YOU HAVE A RIGHT TO CONTROL THE WOMEN AND CHILDREN IN YOUR HOME, AND IF YOU NEED TO USE VIOLENCE TO DO THIS, WELL, WE'LL TURN A BLIND EYE.

... *do as you say*

What about the Church?

In general the churches don't help the present situation of women in society nor her position in the family. It seems somehow that we may still be paying for Eve tempting Adam with the apple!

Most churches would appear to give power to men. The fact that people see God as a man could be why women are excluded from being worthy of the priesthood in the established churches. Nuns and deaconesses do have a role to play in the Church, but we feel it is secondary to that of the priests.

* *Leaving Violent Men*, Binney, Harkell, Nixon. Women's Aid Federation England/Dpt. of Environment 1981. Chapter 2.

This pattern of power extends to the family. Most churches have very clear-cut definitions of what men and women should do in the family unit. In our experience the ideal is the OXO family. Some of us who have stayed within the church as single parents have had to deal with disapproval and condescension. Others have found support, love and understanding.

... be submissive

What has all this got to do with male violence towards women?

This discussion may seem to have taken us a long way away from the problem that this book started with — men abusing women and girls. What has the church got to do with all this, or schools, or what is on the television? We will try to make it clearer with the diagram on pages 64 & 65.

The man in the diagram, like everyone else, has got his own particular problems — he is unemployed, he feels his parents didn't love him enough as a child, and over the years he has got into the habit of drinking too much. On top of these problems though he is under a lot of pressure to behave in typically masculine ways — and to expect his wife to behave in feminine ways. When he feels that she is not doing this, he feels that, as a man, he should do something about it. He, like many men, feels this so strongly that he thinks he has a *right* to be violent.

All through this chapter we have looked at the way our society puts pressure on people to behave in typically feminine or masculine ways. We have all experienced this, but, depending on the culture we come from, we have been affected in different ways.

This is how Janet, who comes from Ireland, describes the pressure on women of her background.

A*s a woman brought up in Ireland by a very traditional and Republican family, a lot of energy was put into maintaining and upholding one's religious and Republican beliefs. The key factor to these beliefs is the woman's morals and values being kept within the culture.*

A lot of emphasis is put on the girl keeping her virginity until she marries. Part of her conditioning is to serve all the men in her family, be it father, brother, uncle or son. As a woman she is encouraged to marry within her own class and area, also, in some cases, to a relative. Although she is taught to recognise the importance of men's education and careers, them being the breadwinner, her own education is actively discouraged. Her role in society as she sees it is to serve her husband, bear him children, particularly sons. She must also rear them to her husband's wishes. She gains little from the partnership itself, although she earns the respect from family and friends if she successfully keeps the marriage together. But if she fails, she is frowned upon, and within some families, she and her kids will possibly be disowned and disgraced.

Sexual rules

As a young woman she is handed down rules from her mother. She must not explore her own body, nor must she speak of or question sexual activities, nor mention the unspoken word. She must not meddle with nature by means of contraception or abortion.

Financial and moral rules

As a family, her culture demands that she and her husband be self supporting. She must ask for nothing, expect nothing from anybody. She is taught to give, not to receive, to care for rather than be cared for. These financial and moral rules can lead to a very unfortunate relationship later on in life. It makes the woman so isolated that she finds it almost impossible to receive from others. If she is to serve her husband totally, she must accept him and his violence and abuses.

PRESSURES ON THE MAN —

You should:

... be tough, like Rambo

... be boss in your own home

... hold the purse strings

You should NOT:

... show weakness

... cry or show your emotions

"Individual Problems"

... UNEMPLOYMENT

... FEELS HE NEVER HAD ENOUGH LOVE AS A CHILD

... SLIGHT DRINK PROBLEM

Your wife should:

... do as you say

... be attractive

... be submissive

... be a perfect housekeeper

N.B. We are not **excusing** individual men for being violent — just trying to show that it is more than an individual problem.

→ INCIDENT → HIS REACTION → RESULT

JUNE
S S M T W T F

WIFE DISAGREES WITH WALLPAPER

"I'm the one who takes the decisions"

NEW BABY ARRIVES

"I'm not getting enough love again"
(Can't express his feelings by talking it over)

BANG!

HOUSE IS DIRTY AGAIN

"I can't let her get away with this"

"People think I'm useless. I'll show them."

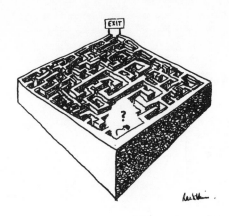

Part Three

Where to go for help.

CHAPTER 5:
PROFESSIONALS, VOLUNTARY AGENCIES AND THE CHURCH

We would like to start this chapter with some basic information on where a woman can go if she is experiencing violence in a relationship. Later in the chapter we have written some personal accounts of what has happened when we have gone for help and some of the attitudes we have come up against.

AGENCIES WORKING AGAINST VIOLENCE AGAINST WOMEN

Women's Aid Refuges

Refuges are set up to provide temporary accommodation for women and children who need to leave a violent relationship. They will also offer advice and information to women who do not need to stay at a refuge. See appendix at the back of the book for ways of contacting Women's Aid.

Rape Crisis Centres

These offer counselling for any woman who has been sexually abused, whether by a stranger or a man she has a relationship with — including a husband, father etc. They also offer counselling to girls and women who are still experiencing the effects of sexual abuse in the past — for example women who are trying to come to terms with childhood sexual abuse.

Rights of Women

Legal advice by and for women.
52 - 54 Featherstone Street, London EC1
01 251 6577

Incest Survivors Groups

Provide campaigning and support groups for children and mothers of children who have been sexually abused. Look out for details of a group in your area.

OFFICIAL AGENCIES
AND WHAT THEY SHOULD DO FOR YOU

Doctors

If you are in a violent relationship, it is a good idea to make sure that your doctor keeps a record of any injuries that you have sustained in case you need legal evidence at any stage. S/he should also keep a record of the effect on your mental health — although beware of them thinking that it is *you* who is causing the problem. Doctors often don't have time to spend with patients, and end up giving tranquillizers, anti-depressants etc. Some women find these make them *less* able to deal with the violence, and to break away from it.

The Police

The police are there to enforce the law — which your partner is breaking

if he assaults you. You are not "wasting their time" if you call them in —
although in some cases you may be wasting your own! In the Leaving
Violent Men survey only 36 out of every 100 women found that contacting
the Police was useful to them. They can:

- Prosecute your partner if he has committed Actual Bodily Harm or
  Grievous Bodily Harm (although usually they don't).

- Support you in prosecuting him, (although they are even reluctant to
  do this, for the amazingly inadequate reason that *some* women withdraw
  charges. We wonder if *policemen* have ever had to share a house with
  someone they are in the process of prosecuting for assault!).

- Very often they will persuade you not to use the Criminal Law against
  your partner at all, but to consult a solicitor and take out an injunction
  which is a civil action – often ineffective – forbidding him from behav-
  ing in certain ways towards you. Sometimes you can get an Exclusion
  Order or Ouster, which will try to exclude him from the home.

- If you have had to leave home because of the violence you can ask them
  to go back with you to fetch essential belongings to ensure that there
  is not a "breach of the peace".

Solicitors

You are likely to need to see a solicitor for a variety of reasons — injunctions,
exclusion orders, separation, divorce, custody and access of children. *It is
worth getting the name of a solicitor specialising in domestic violence from your local
Women's Aid refuge as some are a lot better at dealing with it than others.*

Social Services

Social Services Departments offer different things in different areas, but
you might like to approach them for counselling, help with day care for
your children etc. Again, attitudes vary. Some Social Workers try very hard
to keep families together — when you might be needing to leave home
and make a fresh start. Also, because, quite rightly, they are concerned about
the needs of children, they are sometimes, quite wrongly, likely to under-
estimate the suffering that *women* are going through.

ALL OF THESE AGENCIES SHOULD BE ABLE TO TELL YOU
HOW TO GET IN TOUCH WITH YOUR LOCAL WOMEN'S AID
REFUGE IF YOU SHOULD NEED IT.

ATTITUDES OF PROFESSIONAL AND VOLUNTARY AGENCIES — SOME PERSONAL ACCOUNTS

As we discussed in the last chapter, many people are far too willing to blame women for provoking violence. This, together with society's encouragement of male dominance means that we as women already have it stacked against us.

With professionals it has been common and very easy for us to say "Well, they're the professionals, and they must know what they are talking about", but labelling and stereotyping have been the rule rather than the exception. **We don't need to accept and be put down by a particular professional's explanation of our experience of violence and its effects.**

Even when professionals don't actually blame us for the violence, there is sometimes a tendency to "try to keep the family together at all costs". Even when this is not so, we have found that they don't try as hard as they could to help us overcome our feelings of guilt about "breaking up the family".

Here are some of our experiences of professional, voluntary agencies and the Church. Some people have really helped while others have made things worse. We could go further than that — some have actually been *part* of the problem. By putting us down and not taking the violence against us seriously they have joined the many people in our society who *encourage* men to be violent to women and girls.

Sometimes we find ourselves
labelled by professionals

69

DOCTORS

The sick woman syndrome

I am writing this to all you women out there who like me have found yourself sitting in the doctor's surgery. You don't really know why but you just don't feel well. You have pains that don't go away and headaches. You feel weighed down and depressed, your stomach hurts and you can't go to the loo.

You sit in front of the doctor and he looks at his watch and by now you really feel you are wasting his time. He hardly gives you a second look as you go on about your woes. He is busy writing out a prescription for Valium instead. By now you are already on the other side of his door clutching that bit of paper. Have you then kicked yourself all the way home feeling really angry that you did not get what you had started out for?

Have you ever stopped to think why you don't feel well? Could it be you take everything onto yourself — all the worries and responsibilities? Could it be communication between you and your partner is rather one sided with you giving and them taking? Well, I have discovered something lately and that is to look after someone I had almost forgotten and that is little old me. And do you know something, my aches and pains are not nearly as bad. Makes you wonder, don't it?

Caroline

Stereotyping

I had never liked that psychiatrist. He never liked me. He walked into our flat, the first time we met in his pinstripe suit, his white shirt, the red rose in his button-hole and I felt him look around the room that was both bedroom and living room to us with disdain. He sat as far away from me as he could. I was depressed, unwashed with greasy hair. I was unable at that time to read, print was just meaningless jumble. I became aware under his gaze that I smelt; I felt his distaste from across the room. From that time on I knew he held me in contempt and although in general I agreed with him he still managed to make me feel desperate. Every so often he would say that there was nothing he could do for me and I wouldn't see him again until the next time I took an overdose, and then the process would begin again.

After my first child was born I kept going for four months. Then, although I have no memory of it, I took my last overdose. In hospital, hysterical after my daughter had been taken from me after a visit, I was locked up. He came to see me after I had been sedated. "You mustn't think about ever having another child. Only the strong should have children. I am surprised you have got through four months. There is nothing I can do for you." As he left he said "See you again", and I knew he expected me to go on taking overdoses.

Later when I was in the therapeutic community, I found that he had labelled me as psychopathic and that the prognosis he had made for my life was either self-inflicted death or being a long-term patient in a psychiatric unit. I never did take another overdose. I came out knowing I must never see him again and must find someone else to help me. It took me a year of campaigning and asking before, through the Samaritans, I saw another psychiatrist who immediately took me into the therapeutic community, to somewhere that I felt safe the moment I walked through the door. In that first visit to D__, I felt that he had seen me as a person, as someone of value.

Sarah

I *had an appointment with my doctor. She sat me down and said that my husband had been in to see her and that my appointment to see the psychiatrist had been made, having no idea that they had arranged this.*

Dot

A week after splitting up from my relationship I found out that I was expecting my fourth child — yet another contraceptive failure.

I cracked up shortly after, trying to make my mind up about the baby or an abortion, I was very very confused. I phoned what little family I have and asked (for the first time in my life) if I could come and stay with them for a week with my youngest, they turned me down. I rang my doctor and asked to be fostered for two weeks. I didn't get fostered, but my GP was wonderful. He gave his time, as much as I needed. He didn't push me, he just listened and understood. He didn't flog me off with Valium or the equivalent. He arranged for a psychiatrist to visit me at home to

71

help me find out what I really wanted, what decision I could make and live with. He too was marvellous, gave me a lot of time on his two visits, didn't push me, label me or make me feel bad or uncomfortable in any way.

I am very happy to have received the positive responses from them that I did, because I had enough on my plate to contend with. It was really important not only that they understood but that they were careful to show me they understood.

Sylvia

My doctor had made an appointment to see a psychiatrist on my request. I went to see him to get myself sorted out. I genuinely believed that I was cracking up and I was going mad — destroying my marriage and making his life a misery; what I was doing to my life was low on the list.

My memory of the time is clouded and painful to remember but I will try to sort it out.

On the first visit I told him about my marriage and I seemed to be talking all about my husband and the hurt I was experiencing, but I was putting up a sort of shield or guard, about myself. I don't remember if I told him or I didn't want to tell him, that I had once been taken to a child psychologist, because that would be a background to the present madness. I also don't remember exactly what questions he asked me.

*I think I went for a second visit. I definitely know that he said there was absolutely nothing wrong with me, and that I was blaming myself for everything — that it takes two, and **he** should share in my feeling that the marriage was no good. I couldn't see that at the time. He said I didn't need to see him any more and that all **we** needed was marriage guidance.*

*I don't really know what views he had about me as he was intentionally a good listener and would give me constructive sentences only. All that matters was that his statement of "There's nothing wrong with you" was good enough for me. That led me to see that it wasn't **all me** and much later, that he must take some of the blame for me being the way I was.*

*I felt relief that I wasn't going mad and that all I had been experiencing — the hurt, the confusion, could be explained. It was being done **to** me not **me** causing my confusions.*

SOLICITORS

When I first visited a solicitor, I just told him how things were. I visited him a couple of times and then he said I should make a decision whether to go ahead for a separation or divorce, or to 'put up with things' — as he felt perhaps a marriage guidance counsellor might be more help. I considered this for some time and decided, I felt unwisely for my children's sake, to 'put up' with it. Circumstances later made me regret this decision. When — on the day we left the 'matrimonial home' — I went to see the solicitor, he suggested that I could go back, to as 'things were' or to live there and not look after my husband in preference to staying in someone else's house or in a refuge with conditions not really ideal. This was not really what I wanted as I stated I had thought about my decision and I was NOT GOING BACK. I later changed my solicitor and I feel sure that was the right choice. I think the first did not advise me in the best way. He made me feel that I was silly to have left when of course it was wise. I may have had more material possessions but was very unhappy. Now having gone through the experience of Women's Aid and emerging as happier and with a new home, I feel it was worth the conditions, frustrations etc.

Philippa

I learned the hard way and after two wasted months I found a sympathetic solicitor. The first one I saw was never able to see or even speak to me on the phone — I was palmed off with an articled clerk. Her gender I thought would at least stand her in good stead, but she had absolutely no sympathy. As far as she was concerned I was just another piece of work.

I was asked to make a list of reasons for me wanting a divorce to present to the judge. I dictated to her the very painful mental cruelty I had experienced, and explained how I could no longer put up with the lies. She very quickly dismissed my few, but nevertheless, good reasons for wanting a divorce, saying that, in her experience, it was not enough to "get me through". She said that she very much doubted that the judge would grant a divorce, but she would try, even with such weak reasons. Of course I left that office feeling destroyed and trapped in an unhappy marriage.

A little while after, I visited a neighbour and broke down about my meeting with this solicitor. She told me that a solicitor should work for YOU and be a representative and not make you feel as if she was expecting you to produce a watertight petition. Do you know that you can change your solicitor? If you feel that he or she is not representing you as you would wish you CAN change.

Susan

SOCIAL WORKERS

I have had a very good experience of social workers since the hospital put me in touch with one when my son was ill. I found Jean to be very calm and supportive and she has helped me through my son being ill and my husband leaving home; without her I really would have felt lost being as I also did not have any family to fall back on.

Somehow our family has held together. Even though my husband and I are still separated, we have all grown a lot as people. All this I feel is due to the skill, kindness, patience and time of my social worker.

Caroline

Marriage guidance

Marriage Guidance was a "last resort". My husband didn't want the counselling and escaped it. I went on my own and was helped, by being led gently to a decision.

The counsellor didn't tell me what to think or what to do, but listened and put easy questions to me. Those helped me to an understanding and an eventual decision about how I wanted my life to be from then on.

She did make points, but unbiassed ones, and with so much "advice" coming from friends, relatives and colleagues, her points were very valuable.

Susan

THE POLICE

I phoned the police because my husband was beating me up. They came and after some discussion they told me I was in the wrong because I was holding a brush and was provoking the situation. They asked me if I wanted to press charges but said if I did I was more or less on my own, after they had gone.

Dot

My neighbour called the police in because we were making a row one night when my husband was beating me up. We were outside on the doorstep with her and the police, and she said to the policeman "Isn't there a Women's Aid refuge in .... ?" He said "Yes, there is one, but you can't go in there. Just go back into the house."

I went to meet my ex-husband — which I suppose I shouldn't have done because there was an injunction, and it ended up with a row. My dress was all ripped and torn and he drove me a long way away. The car skidded and he dumped me off, keeping the children in the car and driving off. (He shouldn't have done that because he only had access to them once a week in my house.) I rang 999. The policeman asked to see the injunction, but I didn't have the piece of paper to prove it. He said "You're wasting my time. It's all your fault, you're getting hysterical. If you don't calm down and look after your children you'll have them taken away."

The next day my husband smashed the window. I was too frightened to phone the police. My neighbour did and that time a local policeman came, and he was really helpful. He made arrangements for me to go into the refuge."

Elizabeth

THE COURTS

Here are some extracts from a conversation with Brenda whose child was sexually abused by a baby sitter, who 18 months later was let off with a conditional discharge.

Brenda. Yes and the thing that hurt me most was the fact that these social structures are supposed to help, and that at the end of the day all I got were pieces of paper and pen — nothing positive or constructive was done.

Even the solicitor said yes, they would take it to court, but at the same time it could all be turned round and they could say that my daughter may have provoked him into doing it.

Diane. *And the solicitor thought that was a fair defence — even though he was 18 and she was 9? That's amazing isn't it that it could be even considered as a defence.*

Brenda. He has no right to touch a child! He should know the difference between a child and an adult — OK he might be sexually deprived . . .

75

D. *But then, that's his problem isn't it?*

B. That's right, and you see, all through this my main concern was — if there was nothing to be done about him either through a psychiatrist, or prison or whatever, how many other children would have to be affected — and who else would he tamper with?

My kids did statements for the police.

D. *Was that traumatic for them?*

B. Oh yes!

D. *How did the police deal with them?*

B. Very well. It was the women's unit. They took us down one day to the Police station and the girls went to see the stables, fed the horses etc.

D. *Do you think she has been able to talk about it enough?*

B. Oh yes. In fact if I talk about it now, she tries to block it off. "Oh mum, don't talk about it. Don't keep on about it", and tears come into her eyes. It has been a very emotional stressful time for her, which is why it is so awful for her that the court thing has dragged on so much.

All you get from the court is that there's a waiting list and there's other children that have been through worse. I can see that — but whatever happens to your child is just as bad.

D. *Anyway, there should be more resources all round — you don't want to be in competition with other children.*

B. That's right — but the legal system seems to be more into car thieves than into the violation of people's bodies and the mental and emotional states that they can go through afterwards, which seems really cruel. I just can't understand it.

What I want to know is what are the priorities for professionals these days? For me it seems that if you're not a professional you have to wait in the line — it's like taking a ticket and waiting for them to deal with you — the system stinks.

D. *It can make you very passive can't it? Not that you're passive — but you are being treated like someone very passive — being made to wait.*

B. It's this whirlpool again — and I want to get out of this whirlpool and be happy and contented — and for the kids and me to start living. It could come up again and again — more police, more statements . . .

D. Yes, it makes you understand why parents don't put their children through all that. After all, you can protect your own child now — you just needn't let him come to the house — but you want to protect other children.

B. All these nasty disgusting things should come out in the open so that people would be more careful. I hope there's a better future — I hope this book will help.

THE CHURCH

The church had always been an important part of my life. When I was a child it had given me beauty and love when there had been none at home, and as an adult I remained committed and highly involved. After my husband left I had struggled with, but continued to accept the atittudes of the church towards divorce and sex. Recently a priest questioned me on my acceptance of my life as a single parent. I was asked if I missed sex. I said that I did sometimes. He told me that as it was now, my life was evil and unwholesome — to divorce and marry again would be a sin but less of a sin than remaining as I was. Admitting my sexual loss seemed to him proof of frustration and sexual obsession!

I was so angry that he considered whatever course my life took would be sinful that I began to question the church's position on sexual morality seriously for the first time. I also felt that he would not have spoken to a man in the same way. The imagery of a male God began to disturb me. It is difficult to feel good about God the Father when your own father sexually abused you. I became more and more alienated; although I still believed in God I also felt that in repeating the liturgy I was living a lie. I have left the Church now. It was one of the hardest and saddest decisions I have ever made but realising the position of women in the church made it impossible for me to stay.

Sarah

I used to attend Sunday School and Church quite often when a child, but I did not attend church regularly when teenage or young adult or when married, but I always believed in God.

I did not attend Church after the break up of my marriage until I met someone who told me all about the church he went to, and found that he felt supported and accepted. I attended a supper evening and an invitation service at his church and listened to other people's testimonies. My neigh

77

bours went to church across the road from me and I felt I'd like to go. My younger son went with my friend until I went to a special pentecost service at another city, when I committed myself to God.

Since then I have regularly attended and my faith has grown. It is a very large part of my life and I find that I have joined a large family who accept me as I am but who show care, concern and love. Also I try to give it back to them as well. I hope to marry someone my friend introduced me to who is also a Christian. Both my sons attend church now and I hope they keep to the faith.

Philippa

I am writing this as a Christian, who no longer goes to church. I believe in God and I always will, so I think by writing this I feel a lot of my Christian friends will be very hurt, but I would very much like to write down my feelings about the time I was a regular churchgoer. I have always had a lot of problems throughout my life. This came about because of a very unorthodox beginning. I certainly never thought of going to church, but still there was always something lacking in my life. It was not until my second child was born that I started going — the sole reason being that we were so broke it was one place I could afford to go and the love and concern was certainly there.

It was a very long time before I could make a commitment to God but once I did it was all the way. As my husband and I were not married at the time we felt it was something that had to be put right. This I feel now was a wrong move as we did it for the wrong reasons. We both wanted so much to put things right as by now my husband had become a Christian, but we both did not realise just how many problems we had between us. The church's views on it were once you are married everything will just go away, all my doubts were just blown into the wind and reality kept far away. But how were all these loving, caring middle class people able to identify with the likes of me and the life I had had. I don't blame them — if you have never been there you don't know how it feels. I just could not live up to the pressures even with God's help, and I could not cope with all the guilt. My inferiority complex just got bigger and bigger, my problems larger. Oh how I wanted someone to cry with me for where I was instead of turning it all over to God who I felt knew anyway. It was the human element that was missing, and the emotion that seemed to make everyone so uncomfortable — they did not seem to be able to cope with us all. We seemed to rock their secure little boats.

In the end we begun to lose touch with the real world and went over to a spiritual one, and got deeper and deeper into this. If only someone had stuck their neck out *and told us straight about the mess our lives were getting into instead of setting standards we could not possibly keep! How does one become a perfect mother when one has never been mothered or a father when one has never been fathered? All these pressures were put on us. We felt the only one who understood was Jesus. He knew what it was to be weak and helpless and to feel very alone.*

So my view now is churches can be dangerous when they lose sight of the real world as it is and use their power to make vulnerable people like we were even more so. It takes more than practical help and concern. It takes accepting and a non-judgemental attitude, and above all an awareness of the power they hold.

Caroline

CHAPTER SIX:
REFUGES

Leaving the violent man

It was a Thursday when I decided to leave my husband. I had got up, got my daughter washed and dressed, done all the usual household chores. My husband had actually got out of bed when I returned from the shops. He was filling the football coupon in, asked if I had any money to pay for them. I said no, I had spent it all. This caused him to hit the roof and me. As he was kicking and punching me in the head, I saw my daughter huddled in the corner of the room, really frightened, her poor face showing it all. After he had finished kicking me I felt awful and dreaded leaving my daughter with him while I went to work. But I went to work because it was 'pay day' and he wanted the money. He did not leave a visible mark on me as he knew I had to go to work.

While at work too scared, and trying to hide what had just happened, I decided I would have to do something about it. I remembered I had read a leaflet that came through the door about Women's Aid, what it was there for, and thought I would be the last person to use it. But I just had to get out.

On the Saturday, after a lot of abuse from my husband, I just walked and walked.

I don't know where, but just ended up at the Women's Aid hostel. Just to talk to someone who had experienced what I had been through was a relief. What a totally different place the hostel was to what I had Imagined. Women's Aid gave me a lot of support and self confidence. Without that help me and my daughter would still be living a life of fearful beatings.

Dot

Going into a refuge

Although I had a very good relationship with my family and friends I could not talk to them about the mental, sexual and sometimes violent relationship I was suffering with my husband. There appeared to be no escape until in desperation I contacted the Samaritans. The male voice on the other end asked for some details of my problems but said he could not give me the number of Women's Aid as it was ex-directory but promised to contact them and would call me back. He rang back within 15 minutes and told me how I could contact Women's Aid the following day.

After talking to the workers I realised there *was* alternative accommodation that appeared safe. Although I was apprehensive about going into the refuge I was reassured by the W.A. workers during the phone calls I had with them and it also helped that when they arranged to collect me three of the women already living in the refuge came too.

On entering the refuge I was worried what the other women would be like, it was full of women and children, the place was untidy and I had to share a bedroom with six others, but somehow I didn't care. I was so unhappy and so desperate to leave my husband I felt so relieved to have found the strength to make the move.

Mavis

WHAT IS A REFUGE?

1. A house with an *"Open door"* for any woman who wants to get away from physical, mental or sexual abuse—or who needs to take refuge

81

with a child who is being abused. *You don't need scars or marks as "proof" — you will be believed and your problem will be taken seriously.* (Sometimes there will not be room in your local refuge, but if it belongs to the Women's Aid Federation, they will try to find you a place in another refuge).

2. A place where you can talk in confidence to women who understand. There is always someone there to listen.

3. A safe place to go without involving family or friends — where you can find security and peace of mind.

4. A source of practical help-about everything from finding a solicitor to getting money from DHSS. Refuges are happy to advise women even if they are not needing to come in to stay.

OTHER INFORMATION YOU MAY NEED TO KNOW BEFORE DECIDING TO GO TO A REFUGE

(At the time of going to print this information is correct, but do check out what is written here with a good solicitor. ASK YOUR LOCAL REFUGE TO RECOMMEND ONE as some are a lot better than others at dealing with domestic violence).

Money

You will be entitled to money from DHSS if you do not have a job. This is not much — but is more than many women have been getting from their husbands!

Housing

If you leave home because of violence, and have children, are pregnant or have other dependent relatives then you are entitled to rehousing. This varies from place to place. Although the *law* is the same all over the country, different councils seem to have different versions! Also there is a shortage of council housing everywhere so you may need to be prepared for a long wait. Some women take out injunctions to get their husbands out of the house, but in practice these are very hard to enforce.

Children

Some women are told by their partners that if they come to a refuge they will lose their children. In *general* this is not true—although you will probably need to see a solicitor about your own particular case.

Some refuges have play schemes and workers for the children.

Belongings

If you have to leave your home in a hurry, the refuge may be willing to go back to your house, sometimes with police protection to get your belongings.

Accommodation

Refuges are often crowded—not enough money is spent on them, so basically there are not enough. You will need to share cooking and living accommodation, and may have to share a room with another family. If your local refuge is overcrowded or you are not safe in your own area, you may need to move to another refuge.

Personal freedom

While you are in a refuge you will be encouraged to take your own decisions, although there will be help in talking things over, both from the other women living there and from paid workers and volunteers.

You may leave of your own accord at any time. Many women come to a refuge for a "breathing space", and only stay for a day or so. Some women stay for a while and then go back to have another try. If you do this your decision will be respected—and you will be welcome back if things do not work out. In most refuges women will understand what a difficult thing it is to make a final break—and won't criticise you if you want to have another "go" at your relationship.

As with other helping agencies, if a woman feels "put down" by the attitude of those helping her at a refuge, she has a right to say so. This is an important part of the way refuges should work—they are not official agencies with "clients", but places where women work together as equals against male violence.*

General rules of a refuge

These vary from refuge to refuge, but most will have the following rules:
1. No men allowed in the refuge.
2. No violence towards other women and children in the refuge.
3. Women will be expected to help other women from violent situations — so there are usually rules about answering the telephone and the door.
4. Drugs are generally not allowed, unless prescribed by a doctor, and many refuges do not allow the drinking of alcohol except on social occasions.
5. Many refuges have rules against racism and women are generally expected to make all other women welcome.

General running of a refuge

As women will have left a "boss" at home, the idea is that there should be no "bosses" in Women's Aid. Because of this, important decisions are shared between the women living in the refuge, the paid workers and voluntary "support group" members. Meetings are held regularly so that decisions can be taken, problems sorted out — and everyone has a chance to talk to each other.

Cleaning is usually shared by the women living in the house — often on a rota system.

In many refuges playworkers can be a great help assisting mothers with the welfare of their children, such as safety, schooling, problems coming from their home situation, or from living in the refuge. Play sessions are often available for the children which gives the mothers some free time to discuss their thoughts about the future.

Any refuge worker can always be approached to listen to your views and problems. Many workers and support group members have experienced

* We are basing most of our comments on our experience of refuges which belong to Women's Aid Federation England. (There are also similar Federations in Wales, Ireland and Scotland). Refuges which do not belong to one of the Federations sometimes have quite different attitudes and ways of working.

violent relationships themselves, which often helps women express their feelings more freely.

Here are some more personal accounts of what it is like to live and work in a refuge.

Working in a refuge

I became involved with a refuge and joined the support group. One of the reasons being, my mother had suffered violence from my father, and because refuges didn't exist then, it took her at least 10 years longer than she had wanted, to make the break.

After a couple of years I became a worker, working alongside other women, it was a very new experience, working collectively and sharing skills. Women's Aid principle is to involve all women that is, women in the refuge, support group and workers, in an equal way and decisions are based on this theory.

Women came to the refuge from all walks of life often after suffering for many years—and it still ceases to amaze me how much women had to endure before they came to us.

Most women had tried to get help from other agencies, but the crucial part was missing—the opportunity to have space and time on their own to decide for themselves what the next step was. A refuge fills the most important gap.

The relief that was so visible on women's faces, when they actually realised they were being supported and able at the same time to give support to other women was a joy to see. Women would talk well into the night trying to make sense of their lives, a 24 hour help group, if that's what was wanted.

One of the most exciting parts for me as a worker was to see a woman gain strength and self worth, this was a starting point for her to go forwards and not backwards.

This was not always possible however as the pressure — sometimes impossible — was always high, especially when young children were involved and partners, family, friends and society would rather you were back where you *belonged*'.

Working at the refuge brings back a mixture of feelings.

The one that sums up the worthwhile time I spent there was being allowed to share in a woman's decision to 'make the break' and for her to go out of the Refuge a free woman.

Jenny

Life in a Refuge

I *have lived in the Women's Aid Refuge for 14 months. I feel that the experience I have gained will help me a great deal for building my future. Being able to talk openly has released a lot of stress and tension for me.*

Ever since going into the refuge I have always been interested in helping other women also the children.

Many women find it difficult to unwind, always surrounded by other families but personally I have found it fairly easy to adapt.

By leaving my husband I made myself homeless and unemployed whch hurt very badly, but although it took several months, going into the refuge gave me the strength to get a divorce and to obtain another full time job and hopefully in the near future a permanent place to live.

For the first few months I wasn't interested in having much of a social life outside the refuge but then I started to go out enjoying myself, by visiting my family and friends or going out for a drink, to the pictures or to a singles dance. We generally go out in small groups from the refuge and finding babysitters is not normally a problem.

The help and advice I have been given has helped make life a lot easier for me.

Sharing with other women, good and bad experiences, not having to hold back feelings and being able to laugh again has meant a lot to me.

Mavis

We would like to thank the refuges where some of us have stayed in the past—they have played a really important part in helping us to rebuild our lives. We would also like to thank the two refuges which we have visited whilst writing this book. We have enjoyed these visits and learned a lot. It is good to feel that we had so much in common with other groups of women, and that we are part of the same movement.

CHAPTER SEVEN:
LIVING CHOICES FOR WOMEN —
OR WHAT TO DO WHEN THE FAMILY
ISN'T SO HAPPY

Everything tells us that the "right" way to live is in a proper "family" — husband wife and two children. This can be all right for some people but is not the *only* thing to aim for.

It is worth remembering that we *do* have a choice as to how we wish to live and who we want to share our lives with. We may not be able to choose where we live — for example Buckingham Palace! — but we do have a say and the courage to make our family life a better, more contented and happy one.

The alternative choices we have found are:

- *Living within a female relationship*
- *Living on your own with or without your children*
- *Living on your own with an outside male/female relationship*
- *Living on your own with more than one outside relationship*
- *Living in a refuge or other communal living situation*

Here are some of the things you might want to consider to help *you* make the best alternative for *yourself*. It is nice to be able to value your own time and company. Do you have enough space for yourself to do this??

If you think about it, do you really need to be in a marriage type relationship to be happy? You don't have to rush into another relationship or live with a partner under the same roof until *you* are really sure that this is what *you* want and that *you* are ready for it.

It is not easy, you will find yourself vulnerable, lonely and isolated at times, but you will see the rewards and you and your family will grow and benefit from it.

Make a list for yourself of things that you enjoy, that you haven't been able to do for a long time. These might include: eating a whole box of chocolates, having a bath at 3 am in the morning, with your favourite record on and without having to bolt the door!!!

'GAINS' AFTER LEAVING A VIOLENT RELATIONSHIP

We compiled this list together of what we feel the gains have been from making the break. Some of them we achieved immediately, some took longer and some we had to work hard for.

(There were losses too, which you have already read about earlier in the book — *Chapter 2*).

Being yourself

— *Being able to look at other people without being self conscious about it — for example, in a pub, at a party*
— *Doing things at your own pace*
— *Not having to worry about having to please and having to get it right*
— *Not being dominated*
— *Not having to compete within your own family unit*
— *Being able to get out and about*
— *Being your own boss*
— *Having choice about everyday things*

Deciding for yourself

— Choosing how you spend your time
— Choosing how you spend your money and knowing where your money is going
— Spending as long as you want at the shops
— Not having to explain yourself or your actions
— Choosing the decor for your house
— Having your own friends
— Being able to go on courses
— Being able to give affection to your own children
— Once alone, if you've taken your children, being able to have more decision and responsibility over them and how they are brought up

Gaining your 'rights'

— *Being able to play with your children*
— *Freedom*
— *Sleep*
— *Security of tenure*
— *Not having to keep saying "I've got a headache"*
— *Eating your dinner in peace — not having it thrown over you*
— *Being calm, serene, mellow*
— *Being able to laugh*
— *No more bruises, no more physical pain or mental abuse*

Confidence

— Slowly you get your confidence back
— You are able to experiment and achieve
— Proving to yourself that you are capable
— You gain more determination
— You find your own mind and slowly learn how to act on it

Human luxuries!

— *Being able to menstruate in peace — not feeling dirty about it*

— *Not being frightened to come on*

— *Being able to have a bath alone — without having to bolt the door. Spending as long as you like in the loo*

— *Being able to relax*

— *Being able to wear what you want*

— *Making yourself more attractive*

Here are some of our experiences of what life has been like after the breaking of our relationships, which we would like to share.

A normal day is my children getting up and doing their breakfast (cereal), myself getting up and getting my morning wash, grabbing some breakfast and going to work and the children going to school.

Then I spend my day at work, doing the typing etc., then I walk home and the children are usually in watching TV or playing etc., or playing outside on the green. I usually cook tea, we eat it and we watch TV or I do ironing, washing etc. They chat about friends, or school (mostly school dinners). They, if bored, go to their bedrooms to play and we are usually all in bed for sleep around half past ten.

Phillipa

91

"You feel like you're stuck on a desert island and the rest of the world is sailing by."

Living alone with my children was hard at times. The daytimes seemed alright — somehow they went by, doing bits and pieces, popping in to have coffee with a friend or having a few visitors. To me the house felt "alive" in the daytime. It was once the kids had gone to bed that I found the hours dragged on and I found it very hard to settle down and do anything, though it did get better. When I was on my own at first, several nights a week I would get the kids up, pile them in the back of the car with blankets and drive for about 30-40 miles in circles. The house used to sort of cave in on me and I needed to get out — the loneliness was too much. I managed to get over this and was able to settle down more, either with a book and some music or to watch TV or do some work.

The hardest bit was not feeling guilty about for instance getting the kids out of bed. I learned to tell them and still do, when I'm feeling down or lonely. To tell them that it will pass and that they just have to bear with me rather than trying to falsely put a brave face on for their sake or play with them when I really don't feel like it. Somehow, it seems to make our good times shared even better ones, though they may be fewer.

Getting out in the evenings was hard too. I sometimes had my friend's children to sleep at my house overnight and she had mine in return. Occasionally, I'd pay for babysitters.

Sylvia

As we gain confidence, we feel that we have more and more choice over how we live our lives—and yet, sometimes this choice is limited on every side. Poor housing, lack of transport, money and education all limit what we can do. This is Janet's experience.

Living choices and class

Living choices and class are issues some women aren't even aware of, let alone think about. It's taken me six years to raise my own consciousness to a level of understanding racism and classism, whereby I can now manage to protect myself from some kinds of violence and abuse. I think, if I can assert myself in some situations, I may prevent some nasty experiences.

Being reared in a working class, heterosexist* environment taught me little, but showed me a lot of poverty and struggle. I always knew we were poor, and considered anyone better off than us as posh or snobs. It was understood that the middle class looked down on us and treated us like rubbish, and my fear of being exploited and of my own inadequacies, stopped me mixing with middle class people. I thought it best to stick to my own class where I felt most comfortable. As a teenager I was frightened of making choices or decisions as my culture seemed to make them for me, as they had done for the generation before me. I knew whatever I did I would still be limited. In my late teens I had an emotional relationship with a girl, but was too scared for it to develop any further. Everybody knows what society thinks of lesbians. I had to think of myself, my future, my family, the neighbours, and then, my biggest hang up of all, the church. "Our lady didn't do things like that, she was pure and a virgin" they told me.

So, I did what most girls did, got married and ran away, thinking this would solve everything. Being so naive about life, and ignorant about contraception I was soon landed with three kids and a violent man. Abortion was another side of oppression my culture had given me. My mother used to say, "You make your bed, you lie in it".

However, since I wasn't committed to the marriage, I left after a couple of years. I was beginning to realise I had some options open to me, and I could, with help, choose to make a new life. This was going to be difficult with three kids, no money and no place to live, but I did eventually succeed with the help of Women's Aid. It was at this point I became more aware of class and felt a deep injustice by it all. Being working class meant that because I had no money, or property or saving, I had no "safety net" to fall back on. I used to cry a lot over it, it seemed so unfair. When I came out of the woods, I realised it wasn't only money I needed but some emotional strength and support, and this I could give and receive from

93

my middle class sisters in the Women's movement. I think this is fine, as long as I'm aware and don't forget I also need my working class sisters too, for it is with them I identify and have most in common.

Although it was a relief at last to be able to positively choose relationships with women, it was also a surprise and bonus to find myself growing up within the women's movement and becoming a feminist as well. My opinions and values were changing. This sort of personal growth I wasn't really ready for, I thought, as I was going through the mill, heading towards a place which was to be unfamiliar. As a result of this I found myself a new option. I could now choose whether I wanted monogamous or non-monogamous** relationships with women. This was a new opening, whatever my class, to be able to decide where and how I wanted to live, how committed I would and could be to my kids, my friends or lover/s.

In spite of everything I may achieve, my class still discriminates against me and issues rarely gets resolved. When I open my mouth my culture and my class comes out and, sadly to say, some of my middle-class sisters don't like it – they feel the need to silence me.

Some middle class women have the means – they hold the power, they can help release me and my sisters from struggle, but they don't or won't. They have money, education, social status and this gives them more opportunity to get better jobs and better quality housing. This is the power they are unwilling to share with their working class sisters and because of this power imbalance the working class woman still struggles in poverty. I think, this will remain so until our sisters treat us as equals.

Oh where is this beautiful sisterhood?

* Heterosexist – believing that the only proper form of sexual relationship is with someone of the opposite sex.

** Monogamous – sticking to one sexual partner.

Finally, here are two pieces which show that, though being alone is a struggle, it is also sometimes a positive experience.

Being alone

F irst I had to learn to live alone with my children, then after a few years they began to visit their father for the odd weekend, and I had to learn to be completely *alone. The first time was awful; their father was visiting old family friends, friends who, when we broke up, felt they had to choose one side and had chosen my husband. To fill in the time I decided to decorate the sitting room – a terrible mistake as I spent most of the weekend crying. I tortured myself with memories of our old weekends together – walking by the sea, long meals in their comfortable kitchen, stretching on till midnight. I imagined them all in the kitchen eating and laughing just as it used to be except that I was no longer acceptable! The children returned to find me with red eyes and the sitting room in chaos.*

This was a mistake then, and so, their next weekend away, I organised a hectic social whirl; I had something to do for every minute of the day and most of the night. Although this was an improvement — I didn't have red eyes all the time for a start — I didn't really enjoy anything, and I was exhausted by the end of the weekend. I had been working very hard so that I didn't have to look at myself, my loneliness and my feelings of exclusion from the family and old friends.

Gradually things became better. I got a better mix; I organised myself so that I took advantage of the time socially, but still kept time so that I could learn to be utterly alone. Now, five years on, I love my times alone. I no longer have to think about getting the mix right; the weekends just happen. Sometimes I feel social and sometimes I enjoy being alone. I am not frightened now of silence; when I feel it around me now it feels good.

Sarah

My sixteen months on my own since my husband left have been very hard. I have three small children and at times felt I am really not going to make it. Yet, I feel I have grown such a lot as a person in that time. I am more confident and secure, and feel that I have a life of my own now, where, once I was submerged in my husbands life.

The love and understanding I received from the women's course I joined, taught me just how much support can be gained from other women, and I feel now that I am much more self-reliant.

It has not been easy, and looking back, it is not a route I would have chosen for myself. But now that I have come through the worst of it, I am a much stronger happier person, looking forward to doing things with my life.

Caroline

CHAPTER 8:
NEW RELATIONSHIPS WITH MEN

What we _do_ want from relationships with men

In the last chapter we talked about choices – *e.g.* the choice of living alone or with another woman. Many of us would choose to live with men, but only if we can be sure of not ending up in another bad situation. So we began to think about what we do and don't want from relationships with men – and what we are definitely not prepared to put up with!

Here is our list of unacceptable behaviour – which may seem long . . . . but is a lot shorter than our original!

Around the house

- Thinking that the woman's place is in the home – but that the man can come and go when he likes.
- Not taking an equal role in the running of the house.
- Saying "I can't do it – you're better at it than me!"

Money

- Making women feel they are lucky to have money "given" to them from men.
- Not being able to use your own phone – having to ask permission.
- Booby trapping the phone by putting cotton on the dial.
- Landing up in arrears without being told.

Trust

- Not trusting me.
- Meeting me if I'm ten minutes late home from work.
- Having to bring shopping receipts home.
- Always accusing me of affairs.
- Not trusting my judgement.
- Lying.

Sexual

- Sexual abuse.
- Being raped.
- Expecting sex if I didn't want it
- Being there only for his sexual needs.
- Thinking sex will make everything better.
- Refusing to use contraceptive.
- Sleeping with other women.
- Threatening to leave if woman becomes pregnant.

Childcare

- Not wanting to take an equal share with the children.
- Not cuddling or kissing the children.

- "You had the kids you look after them".
- Sexual or physical abuse of the children.

Violence

- Cruelty – mental or physical.
- Using their power to make me do anything that I don't want to do.
- Having to cook a meal very late at night.
- Throwing things about.
- Drinking with violence.
- Threatening behaviour.
- Slagging me.
- Bullying.
- Swearing at me or the kids.
- Always wanting to be the boss.

Taking away our right to be ourselves

- Not being allowed out.
- Not letting me have friends.
- Not accepting my need for women's company.
- Making me feel less important because I am a woman.
- Never listening to what I want.
- Not allowing me to have an opinion.
- Not accepting me as I am – only as the person he wants me to be.
- Expecting me to look nice all the time.
- Saying "You don't really think that!"
- Not understanding that I get tired.
- Lack of respect.
- Not allowing me to be alone or quiet.

Others

- Embarrassing me in front of friends.
- Being happy to stay in a relationship which they don't care about.
- Selfishness.
- Unable to accept others feelings.
- Blaming me for things which are wrong with him.
- Making out the woman is sick.
- The assumption that they are more important.
- Arrogance.
- Pig-headedness.
- Putting down my consideration for others.
- Belittling/ridiculing.

Perhaps an interesting question to ask whilst reading this list is – "Would a man show this sort of behaviour if he really had respect for women as equal human beings?"

A Personal view

I think men always think of themselves, not what other people think. If it's OK by them then it should be OK by you. *e.g.,* I have known a man for a number of years as a friend, but now I'm on my own he seems to think that because he's offering himself to me, I should be glad and take it. He hasn't stopped to think about his wife and children at home – the time he spends with me he could be with his family.

Fiona

"After Eights"

Some of us were chatting about how you could see in advance whether a man was likely to be violent, when Dot told this story.

My little girl and I were having a meal with a bloke who had taken me out a few times. Sally, my little girl, wasn't that hungry, and didn't eat all the first course. But when it came to the pudding, of course she wanted ice-cream. I said "Yes, that's all right" but the bloke was looking a bit annoyed. Anyway the ice-cream came, and it was one of those huge ones – three great big portions – and, of course, she couldn't eat it. I didn't mind too much, but he must have been thinking that she shouldn't have had it in the first place. Anyway, the bill came – and with it three "After Eights". Of course, her eyes lit up, and she said "Can I have one Mum?" "Of course you can", I said. Anyway, that was it! He just threw the money across the table (I didn't want him to pay anyway), and stormed out of the restaurant. So that was it!

One of the problems in forming new relationships with men is that a lot of the things which we feel often lead to violence, (and which in any case we are not prepared to live with), are considered "normal" – as this account of meeting men in pubs shows.

Danger signs to look for in men

When a woman meets a man, one who appeals to her she can see straight away what type he is. He may be good looking, a good dresser, full of confidence – a true sterotype he-man, one who makes you go weak at the knees, a man anyone would be proud of . . . . or should we? Men like this may be the sort we should steer clear of. I must admit that not all "he-men" turn out to be violent, but there is a strong chance of it. In fact, if you think about it, the very things that make him "the man of your dreams" are likely to be the first danger signs.

The most likely place to meet men is in a pub or maybe at a party or work. Wherever you meet, beware of the man who first smiles and puts his arm around you when he buys you a drink. Next he will ask if he can sit with you. When you go to buy a drink he grabs your glass, diving up to the bar. In the meantime he starts to get closer to you – too close so that he's almost on top of you. When you go off to the loo you might see someone you know who starts to talk to you. You go back to your table and he looks cross; even if you talk to the friend you went out with you can see that he wants you on your own. He tries to attract your attention, so he has his wish. He starts to brag about what he does, where he's been, what car he drives. Then he starts to pull the pub apart, saying he usually goes to better. Then he asks "Would you like to come for another one with me?" and, like many women who want some excitement, you decide to go off – if sensible, in a foursome.

By the time you get to another pub he leads you in with an arm or by your hand, sits you down, goes off to the bar, just as if you have had a relationship for ages. As the night draws on he gets to asking you how you will get home, trying to find out where you live, if you are on your own etc.

Another danger sign is that if you decide to say goodnight without arranging to see him again or letting yourself be driven home, he starts to say you are lucky he isn't like other blokes who would have got mad because you let him buy drinks all night. Or he might go on and on, saying its a shame how someone as nice as yourself should be on your own – anything to win your trust. He then may try to show you up in a pub full of people, then if you resist he walks off. There may be something that you like about him though, and, like a magnet, can't pull yourself away. You feel you wish to find out more – maybe he will be all right. If you haven't been out for some time you are at risk because you feel he may be the one and only man who will talk to you and have an interest in you. Somehow you let him dominate you without realising it – and you end up going home with him.

At this point I usually get a taxi, but that's me. Sometimes I have let them take me home if I feel I can trust them, but after one incident, I now ask to be dropped off close to my home and never invite them in. Anyway, if you agree to be taken home, somehow you lose your friend to the other man or you all go home to one place with some takeaways.

You start to kiss. If you are attracted to each other it feels great. You sit and have a cuddle, you talk, have some more drink. Then he starts to get hand trouble up your blouse, up your skirt; you tell him to get off; you stand up – or try to; you are gasping for air. If you are lucky you break away and say "I'm not a one night stand – not that easy. If he is decent he says "Sorry" and explains that he thought you were! If he's a decent sort of chap he says he will go and asks "Will I see you again". Otherwise, he might try to force you to have sex, because he thinks – you had his drinks, you let him drive you home, and because you were in a pub you were out asking for it. He then starts to throw abuse at you. Then you realise you have a big dangerous problem on your hands trying to get rid of him.

It's always best to leave a bloke at the pub, arrange to get to know him before taking him home. I find it hard to let a bloke get close to me now, and after what's happened to me, I'm sure when I meet a man I can tell the dominators because of the mannerisms. Most men are Jack the Lad when they meet women. I find when they have friends with them (men) they show off, flirt, trying to attract your attention. On their own they are loud, trying to attract attention to themselves.

The best way of getting what you want is to talk to the bloke first if you can without trying to be dominating. If he's the type to be equal or your type, he may be for you. I've only found one. He was all that I thought I wanted, but I blew it because I forced things on him too soon – like the men I'm trying to avoid! So now it's me to watch as well as them. I still fall for the violent types, but have learned to stay away. Even though they are gift wrapped they have DANGER written all over them, and like rock, all the way through.

Elizabeth.

WHAT WE *DO* WANT FROM RELATIONSHIPS WITH MEN

Two women have written about what they would be looking for in new relationships.

1. *TRUST* – between both man and woman. The comfort that comes with the knowledge that you know you can trust your partner and they you.

2. *RESPECT* – for each other, for mental, physical and general well-being. Consideration goes with this too, for each others views, ideals, goals and achievements – also interests and religion.

3. *SUPPORT* – in times of weakness and or depression – in matters concerning the children, work and home maintenance.

Susan

I *would like a relationship with a man who could have a great deal of the following qualities — understanding, patience, kindness, someone who will be understanding to my children, who will help me in the house, cheer me up when I feel low, someone to laugh with, and who will have a listening ear and who will share their problems with me. A generous caring man, who would not be reliant on drink. Someone who will be affectionate and have self-respect but who can care for others and not just for himself. If I had this from a man I would be loving, caring, affectionate as well.*

Phillipa.

What makes relationships so hard to sort is the way that what we want and what we don't want is sometimes mixed together in the same man.

R omance hit me when I was seventeen. I had been out with boys before but I had not responded, and they had always told me I was frigid. Then I met the man who would become my husband. He excited me physically, emotionally, intellectually, in every way. I admired the assured way he seemed to know his goals and worked towards them. I felt comfortable because we shared a religious background. Within two weeks we were lovers and it all started. We went to the theatre a lot, went motor cycling, hill walking, read poetry together. There seemed to be nothing that we didn't do together. Then, after five years, we married and all that stopped. We were both students and somehow became rivals. I felt I would be the one to lose, and became pregnant as an escape.

Twenty years on I feel a single parent *and* married. I am happy in most ways living on my own and acknowledge myself free to enter another relationship. I can truthfully say I would not want to live with him yet he still claims a part of me. To define why is difficult and complex, but part of it certainly is desire. And although desire is the last thing I think of now when he visits the children, I am aware that it is there, dormant.

I am not proud of these feelings for it seems to show how much I am stuck inside a relationship that is finished. Why am I not capable of going on like others, renewing and rebuilding that part of my life?

I suppose it is because there is more than this. Those years before we married he put no labels on me. I just was myself and he wanted me. No other man has ever done that.

And so he penetrated me deeper than sex, deeper than any other passion I have ever felt, apart from my children, and the seeds he impregnated within me remain inside me potent. And unless I ever meet a man who can let me be that free they will remain potent.

Sarah

Conversation with Lorna

Lorna had been living for fifteen and a half years in a violent marriage when she approached Women's Aid an decided to leave. After a while she became a paid worker in a refuge and remarried. We talked to her about what the differences were between her first and second marriages, and how she had approached forming a new relationship.

Lorna. I met my husband through Gingerbread. There were 4 men and 10 women who went out as a group and I am still friendly with some of them. At that time you had to have custody of the children to join so they all had kids.

Susan. *Can you just be friends? I have been to Gingerbread and felt smothered.*

L. When I first met my husband, I didn't want a relationship. He didn't push himself. No-one was pushy, jealous or demanding. I wasn't conscious at the time of setting limits on the relationship.

Diane. *Was Mike the first bloke you went out with?*

L. No, I went out with Mike and someone else. They both knew. One was much younger. The main practical problem with Mike and myself was that we each had four children! At the beginning we took everything so slowly. We did everything as a group, but we ended up together because we both loved dancing. He didn't just take me home, he took others too – and he didn't always drop me off last!

At that time I didn't trust anyone anyway. I went to Gingerbread for companionship.

(General discussion on Gingerbread, different women had different experiences).

S. *There's one good thing about Gingerbread – if a man is giving you problems you can talk to someone on the committee.*

L. It's a good idea to make ground rules. I was pretty clear about not wanting a relationship at that time.

Sylvia. *But if that was my ground rule I'd be kidding myself – I've never been happy, not for one day without a relationship. I've never given myself that opportunity.*

L. One of my problems was that after 15½ years of marriage it was really difficult just knowing what to do when I went out. I always remember going to a disco with some other girls and a man offered to buy me a drink. I rushed back to my friends and said "What shall I do?" They said "Go on . . . . if you want him to say Yes!" So then I went back and said "Yes, I would like a drink!"

S. *Yes I hate all that dating game business.*

L. But generally, because we went out in a group it was just good fun.

D. *What other ground rules did you make?*

L. If he'd started making plans then it would have been 'bye bye' (Mind you if you say too much it can be a come-on).

S. *In one situation I was in everything was just friendly and then I made the mistake of sleeping with the bloke. It changed everything . . . . it wasn't just a friendship after that.*

Caroline. *Sometimes it can help.*

L. I find it strange that we assume that because there is sex it has to be serious.

Sylvia. *There are some men you can have a friendship with and sleep with occasionally, without there being an entanglement.*

L. Another ground rule (although it was something that we just accepted without even talking about it), was that he didn't have to be possessive about my time. With Women's Aid I was out at all hours. I would say "I can't go out tonight and it would be "fine, no problem". I didn't have to explain.

C. *If that was me I'd begin to think he didn't care . . . .*

L. It was such a contrast with my first husband. He was so domineering. I wanted FREEDOM!

D. *How did the relationship develop?*

L. We started going out alone to "test places" for the rest of the group. We were both so shy, we needed this as a sort of excuse. Then after about 9 or 10 months we started spending weekends together, then I introduced him to my family . . . . put my L plates on his car . . . .

I remember during this time we were out with some other people, and he said "You and Mary buy a drink. That really meant a lot to me because that was the sort of thing my ex would never allow. (Mind you I was disappointed on that occasion, because the blokes at the other end of the bar insisted on buying drinks for us – I was so mad!)

I also admired him a lot for the way he was bringing up his family.

Sylvia. *In some ways, blokes who are looking after children give you a sense of security. There is a good reason for not living in each other's pockets, and you're not always worrying about why they're not available!*

L. Later on we went on holiday for 2 weeks, then we started living together and eventually after 4 or 5 years, got married. It takes so much longer to trust if you've been damaged by a previous relationship. My ex really had no concern for me, so when things went right with Mike I was waiting for something to go wrong! I can remember he looked after all the kids for me when I went to my first Women's Aid conference. I had a really good time, but kept thinking about what might be going wrong at home, but when I got back he was up a ladder decorating, the kids had had a great time . . . . everything was fine.

C. It's a real danger isn't it giving up your interests?

L. It was important to me that at the end of my first marriage I was helped to see by a Marriage Guidance Counsellor where some of my own vulnerability lay. I had had a very domineering father and had gone straight into a relationship with a very domineering husband. It was important not to fall into that trap again. With Mike I had something completely different. For example, my first husband would never let me dance with anyone else. At first I thought that was protective and nice, but now I see it as part of his possessiveness and jealousy.

I was very underconfident in my first marriage. I remember him taking me to a restaurant one night, and as soon as we got inside I was too frightened to walk in and asked to leave. I got a good hiding for that when I got home. Exactly the same thing happened with Mike – we got there, and I couldn't face going in. He just said, "Never mind love" and <u>accepted</u> how I felt.

Driving is another example of how different things were. My ex said I was too thick to drive. Mike taught me and was so patient – he kept telling me "You can do it." It was Mike who persuaded me to take the job with Women's Aid when it was offered me. He's not even jealous of other men. The chap I was going out with in the early days turns up every now and then and we go out to lunch – and that's ok. Mind you I used to push him a lot in the early days to see if he would get angry.

Sylvia. *What about chemistry? Occasionally I have met someone who is really nice, has offered me the world, but I haven't been in love, so it hasn't worked.*

L. At first I wanted something in common-companionship. The attraction came after – though it is important – even now we still always kiss each other goodnight.

Another thing we've never done, is gone into our previous relationships – we learned more about this from the kids than from each other.

C. How long did the trust take to build up?

L. About four years, I kept worrying that things would change if we got married.

D. Do you know a lot of women who have gone through the refuge and formed good, equal relationships.

L. Not really. It's very difficult. It's difficult for the women working there too. It can put a pressure on a relationship. *Any* man has *some* dominant attitudes and it can make you very critical. This can make a relationship better in the end though, if you can work things through and improve them. You can both see things in a different light.

The important thing for any woman entering a relationship is to build confidence in yourself – and to find out what is good for *you.*

Lorna's comment about *any* man having dominant attitudes is really important. When we made our lists earlier on about what we did and didn't want from relationships it seemed as though we were looking for perfection . . . . and that could take some time!

Perhaps the most important thing is to look for someone who is prepared to work things through and to question the pressures on him to be a typical macho man. Even the man in our diagram on page 64 would have got on better if he had kicked the pressures on him out of the window instead of taking it out on his wife.

Another thing that has come out really strongly in our discussions is that as women we are under a lot of pressure to *expect* and accept dominant behaviour from men. We have caught ourselves fancying the strong dark handsome types, thinking its a bit odd if men do the cooking – have had a laugh about the sort of aprons they wear . . . . .

This isn't the same as saying women are to *blame* for male violence we hope we've spent long enough knocking that idea. We do, after all, live in the same world as men (although sometimes it *does* seem as though we live on another planet!) so perhaps its not surprising we have got some of the same pressures on us too.

Although this chapter has been about relationships with men – a lot of what we have said – especially about equality and respect applies if we choose to have sexual relationships with women. We would like to say that when two women have a relationship everything is automatically fine, but even in our relationships with women, we still need to look at our attitudes and behaviour – and work against possessiveness dominance and jealousy and towards respect, equality and love.

CHAPTER NINE:
THE WAY THAT WE BRING UP OUR CHILDREN

If we are working towards more choice over how we live our lives as women, and a more equal relationship between women and men, how does this affect the way we bring up our children?

Our children have gone through a lot and we feel they deserve the best we can give them. We want them to grow up looking for respect and equality in relationships – and with enough confidence and love to achieve this. We want them to have a strong sense of their own rights – and the rights of others. We also want them to be able to "see through" all the ways that they are being stereotyped in typically masculine and feminine ways – because we feel that if they can see what is happening they can make their *own* choices.

We feel that in this way, not only are they less likely to be abused – and abusers – but they will be able to contribute to the struggle for a world where *any* kind of violence or exploitation is unacceptable.

CHILDREN'S RIGHTS

Here are some of the rights which we felt were important to our children. Some of us worried about where our rights finished and our children's began – also about getting the balance right between parental guidance and the rights of children. Anyway here is what we came up with.

Children have a right

To safety

- To be free from any form of violence or violation
- To have safe parents
- To be able to trust their parents
- To expect the adults in their lives to take responsibility for them – but to allow them responsibility too.

To self expression

- To say "No"

110

- To say what they are feeling
- To voice an opinion – especially about things concerning them
- To cry or snivel
- To be able to talk to their parents
- To question adults

To love

- To cuddle the adults who care for them, and show their affection physically
- To be loved and wanted
- To be valued for who they are
- To know who their natural parents are

To be respected

- To be listened to
- To privacy
- To independence
- To have time to themselves
- To be allowed as much dignity as adults
- To expect equality
- To choose their own friends whatever class of society

To learn

- To develop at their own pace
- To make mistakes
- To be inquisitive
- To play
- To act naturally – not always the way their parents want them to
- To ask questions

- To make a noise – (sometimes!)
- To be free to find out who they are
- To be free to play with girls and boys toys without distinction

This piece expresses very well the difficulty a lot of us have in trying to get it right for our children.

CHILDREN'S RIGHTS

*A*s a parent with two daughters and a son I'm trying to bring them up to believe in themselves, their worth as individuals and to love and be loved in the way they want. It's difficult to offer them the security of my love without dominating them totally. Sometimes I silence them with my anger, and my refusal to hear "No" also oppresses them. I find it hard to balance out their rights against my rights.

The four of us need and want different things. Because I tend to silence their "no", they tend to go along with me and say "yes", because that's what they think I want to hear. I think this can make them very vulnerable and not stand up for their rights later on.

Janet

STEREOTYPING

Children's toys help stereotyping

Thinking back to our discussion in chapter 4 about how the pressures on men and women to be typically masculine and feminine is often at the root of violence, we began to think about ways in which we could bring up our children in less stereotyped ways. Here are some of our ideas.

- *Less violence on TV, e.g. war films.*
- *Equal opportunities in schools e.g. in Craft, Science, and Sport.*
- *More work in schools on relationships and sex roles etc. Less on how families should be and more about how they are.*
- *More awareness of attitudes in school towards boys and girls, e.g. less "I want four strong boys to move these chairs" and "Girls in one line and boys in another".*
- *Assertiveness courses for teenagers.*
- *In the home – men should set an example by being involved in childcare and housework – and women, by doing more D.I.Y. etc.*
- *Boys and girls should be encouraged to do the whole range of household jobs.*
- *Pink for girls and blue for boys should be abolished!*
- *Boys and girls should be given equal choices over toys and clothes.*
- *Boys and girls should be encouraged to cry and show their emotions.*
- *Dressing up should be OK for boys as well as girls.*
- *Girls should not always be seen as the carers.*
- *We should encourage girls and boys to stick up for themselves without being aggressive.*

In the world generally we should be working towards a peaceful and loving lifestyle.

A lady at work.

A drunk man at home.

We asked a 9-year old girl to draw her image of a man and a woman and to draw what they might be doing during the day.

113

Men, Children and Possessiveness

This is a discussion held one afternoon which we decided to tape at the time. After reading the transcript we agreed that we wanted it printed the way it happened. We hadn't at the time decided to talk about possessiveness and it's interesting that that was the path it took. We didn't end up with any answers about how far we should go in protecting our children, but it did raise the issue for us.

Louise. My little girl's father wanted to be with her when she was ill, but I pushed him away. I felt he was putting pressure on her.

Caroline. Yes but wouldn't you want your husband to try to help get treatment?

L. I am capable of getting this for myself.

C. I was resentful of my husband – he left it to me – I didn't have the choice.

Diane. Yes but Louise didn't think that man was the right one for that child.

L. Also it was something about the relationship between me and my daughter – we know each other inside out. There isn't anyone who can get in between us. I am really possessive – I can let my son go more. I don't like her cuddling up to anyone else. It's perhaps because she's ill.

Fiona. That's how my husband was with me. It put a lot of pressure on me.

My father was very protective towards me. I knew my Dad more than my Mum. When my Dad died the whole world collapsed around me. Then my husband came along and I put everything into him. Perhaps because he's a similar sort of person. Then my daughter came along and he doesn't like the bond that she has with me.

If the three of us were watching telly she's not allowed in the middle. She's allowed the other side, but my husband's got to be there by me.

With the milkman – I bent down to pick something up, and the milkman looked down and my husband felt that he was looking at me – he's that possessive.

He would take me anywhere – because he wanted to be with me. When I was younger I thought it was great, now that I've got four children of my own – no!

Jenny. I can relate to what Louise has said, because my daughter and I are very

114

close. There was a stage when she was inseparable from me, and that made me realise that I wasn't doing this child any good.

Louise. But you don't mean it in a possessive way – its more in a caring way.

What do other people feel about the protectiveness bit – either with men or with children?

Amy. *I don't like it.*

Brenda. Neither do I.

Sylvia. *I've got two daughters and the little one is the one that's been ill. I've got that kind of bond with her – I find it very difficult to let her go with anyone, but I've been forcing myself. There have been problems as well, when I worry about her dad walking off with her, but putting that to one side, I find it very difficult to let anyone look after her. I did let friends look after her for a week while I went on holiday, but when I got there I just cried.*

Sarah. I find it difficult to leave my child when he's ill – "I'm the only one who knows what to do" etc., but when he's well, there's never been any problems with him staying with people. But I have my daughter who has refused to go to school. In the end I saw an educational psychologist. I had to go to school with her – it was as if a bit of her had got stuck at the age of two, and I had to treat her as if she was going to playgroup – staying there and just going out for cups of tea etc. That arose from a sort of crisis. She was all right – but she always thought her father was coming back. I don't know whether she thought that I was going or something. It's very hard because a part of you is trying to protect them from these feelings, and another bit is saying – this isn't right for a child of that age to be so clingy.

Jenny. *Yes it was the same with my daughter. It was no good saying – "Right, you just have to be independent . . " I just had to go back to square one with her – be with her all the time and treat her like a young child again.*

Sarah. I was fortunate in that the educational psychologist we saw, saw the head and the teachers – the school found all this very difficult to cope with, so it was lucky that there was someone in authority who was liberated enough to see that that was what was needed. So I had to sit cross legged in assembly!

Diane. *I think we should break now, but its interesting isn't it that sometimes things that seem quite good like being protective, can sometimes be part of the inequality and the threats to your rights, and I think that's why men are so confusing – and why our relationships are confused.*

Jenny. I think that it's interesting that Sarah and I having similar childhood backgrounds (sexual abuse) have similar problems with our children.

Sarah. *At least our daughters could express how they felt.*

Louise. I haven't experienced that (sexual abuse as a child) but I've still got that same fear. I don't mind giving her her freedom as long as she's with her brother – although he's younger.

Jenny. *Teenage boys in the refuge tend to be very protective towards their mothers.*

Louise. My little boy is towards me as well – if anyone gets near me he goes and kicks them.

C. *Yes my little boy does that too.*

Susan. My little girl too – but then she doesn't see men touching me much so she doesn't know what's going on.

Louise. *It's silly that I feel that my boy toddler being a boy will somehow survive – whereas I don't with my little girl even though she's much older.*

Diane. It's interesting to see how those feelings about little girls – that they need more protection etc. – have oppressed us as women.

CHAPTER TEN:
WHAT WE CAN DO FOR OURSELVES

RECOGNISING OUR RIGHTS ENJOYING
TRUSTING
VALUING OURSELVES
LOVING
WORKING EXPRESSING
FIGHTING BACK CREATING
SHARING
FRIENDSHIP WITH WOMEN
LEARNING
SELF-RESPECT

We wanted to end the book on a really positive note – because although breaking away from violence is a real struggle we KNOW IT IS WORTH IT IN THE END.

We start this chapter with a list of some of the things that have helped us, some of which we have already discussed earlier in the book. We follow this with personal accounts of four areas which we think are really important. VALUING OURSELVES, FRIENDSHIP WITH WOMEN, FIGHTING BACK. (Refusing to behave like a client or a victim), and OUR RIGHTS.

117

THINGS WHICH HAVE HELPED US

1. Sharing our troubles with a friend who you feel may understand or lend an ear – but also listening to them because each person has their own problems.

2. Finding other women to talk to who have been through similar experiences.

3. Forming close friendships with other women, so we are not to dependent on men for emotional support. FRIENDS ARE IMPORTANT AS WELL AS PARTNERS.

4. Learning to trust other people, which can mean choosing carefully who we confide in – if someone lets us down this really knocks our trust again.

5. Learning not to blame ourselves. Working hard to get rid of feelings of guilt over breaking up our marriage or relationship.

6. Being KIND to ourselves – trying to think of our good points and what we have achieved. (This can be very hard).

If you're depressed try to think of your 10 best points

7. Not bottling up our feelings about the past – they are real and need to be worked through in order to go forward.

8. Learning to express and release our bitterness, resentment and hatred.

9. Thinking about what WE want out of life – leisure? Training? Friendships? Relationships? Work? Enough money to support ourselves without a man?

   Working to get what we want – whilst realising that it's not always *our* fault if we can't get it. (Perhaps the right partners just aren't around . . . . or there just aren't the training and work opportunities for women where we live.)

10. Taking our spiritual needs seriously. Within our group we have done this in different ways, for example:
    ● Working on finding out who we are
    ● Finding spirituality within ourselves
    ● Forming close friendships with others
    ● Acknowledging God
    ● Seeking a higher power

11. If we want to form new, close relationships – with men or women – being clear about what we want and don't want – and learning to ask for it.

12. Working for EQUALITY in relationships.

13. Joining groups for support. Groups which have helped us are:
    ● Women's groups
    ● Church groups
    ● Assertiveness training courses
    ● Second Chance to Learn, Wider Opportunities for Women courses
    ● Gingerbread
    ● Women's Aid

14. Working out what our rights are – and asking for them.

15. Working with others against male violence – and violence of any sort. Some have done this through organised groups – *e.g.* Women's Aid, the Peace Movement. Others have worked on a day to day basis against all the attitudes which cause violence.

VALUING OURSELVES

Learning about your own self value, learning to like yourself and to have self respect, I would put all together as the beginning of rebuilding.

This is the road to a new life. For me it has led to a deepening of my faith in God and a new understanding of the way I was persecuting myself.

When you begin to value yourself and know you are worth a better life it is freedom of the best kind.

TRYING TO VALUE YOUR OWN TIME AND COMPANY is hard work at first! Making time for yourself is of course very difficult when you have children, but the odd half hour, at first, pampering yourself does wonders as a morale booster. Even if it's a long soak in a hot bubble bath on your own! In time you will be able to, with friends's help, grab a shopping expedition on your own and the odd evening ut. But this is a dangerous time, when falling back into an unwanted relationship is all too easy.

The hardest of all is valuing your own company. Long lonely evenings are hard to bear and your mind can play tricks with you. Turning to drink, also sinking into depression are two of my experiences. There's no easy answer, you have to come to your own way. Using your past interests and hobbies is refreshing, or making plans for yourself are positive mental plusses.

If you achieve self-respect, then avoiding repeating the pattern is taken care of.

Susan

Clearing the cupboards

> *The cupboards are clear.*
> *I have spent all summer clearing them,*
> *Swept out the cobwebs,*
> *Washed the marks from the walls,*
> *Arranged and rearranged the furniture.*
> *Ruthlessly I reassess the past.*
> *Letters are difficult; I keep them still,*
> *Will keep them, maybe, until I die.*

The pottery that I was given
The cats have broken, piece by piece;
I wept, but live without them easily.
Clothes are simple, I always
Chose to please another;
Now they slip unheeded from my wardrobe.
I bury them neatly in black plastic bags.

In the garden the ivy begins
To climb the high fence.
I shall buy a honeysuckle
In the spring.
I walk my garden's boundaries.
This is my territory.
I define it.

Sarah

FIGHTING BACK

Very often people talk of "Battered women". This can give the impression that women who experience violence are simply passive victims — women with a problem. It is important to see ourselves as women who *can* be strong, and can take a very *active* part in deciding what to do with our lives.

The first step in fighting back can be in taking the decision to leave a violent relationship in the first place.

Knowing what you want

To me, this is a very important matter to sort out. Right from the discovery that "something is wrong" in your marriage, it really means the difference between insanity and a decent future.

I certainly was able to think clearly and felt a weight had been lifted once I had decided what I wanted out of my life. Of course the decision was difficult and a long time coming. There are plenty always willing to give advice, but although they mean well they don't really help you. Once you feel it's "right" and in your heart you are released, then that gives you the strength to go forward.

Susan

This story, told to us by a refuge shows a woman *literally* fighting back.

One woman had travelled all the way down from one end of the country to another to escape her violent husband. She had been crying for the whole journey. She got off the train with her baby and luggage only to be propositioned by a man – "You look as if you need a bed for the night".

She screamed at him and chased him out of the station, followed by a policeman and the stationmaster. A porter looked after her child and bags. Afterwards the stationmaster put her in the taxi and said "Take her anywhere she wants to go!

The woman in this story seems to have found an energy that she may not have known she had – and this is what countless other survivors of male violence have found. Sometimes we have to get angry to find this energy – in which case we should value the anger – and not allow ourselves to become embarrassed or ashamed of it. It may not be how we've been brought up to behave – and some people – perhaps like the stationmaster – may even be slightly amused by it. For us though it can be a powerful force in surviving the effects of violence.

This poem continues the theme of valuing our emotions rather than thinking they are silly or embarrassing. Belonging to a women's group, and spending time with other women can help us to do this, and can be an important part in our struggle to live in a way that *we* choose.

Crying

> *When I remember our group*
> *I shall remember Sarah, crying as she reads her poems.*
> *Because of Sarah,*
> *Crying to me has become a sign of strength,*
> *Of struggle, of growth.*
> *Of power.*
> *Power to fight,*
> *To work through the unspeakable,*
> *To give it a voice,*
> *To tell us – so that she and we will know and understand.*

122

It is a sign of anger
At the way others saw her crying,
And, judging by their own cool, rational values,
Thought she was a useless victim
And locked her up.
Her crying
Helps us to value our own emotions,
To make our own rules,
To struggle together.

Diane

For some of us the struggle has been not only against the violence itself, but against what it has done to our health. This poem tells of Sarah's recovery from mental illness – and of how she had to encounter yet another struggle when she left hospital.

W hen I was a child a bible story that really intrigued me was the account of Jesus raising Lazarus from the dead in Chapter 11 of the Gospel according to St. John. How could the people that witnessed this miracle betray Christ to Caiaphas, the high priest? How did they justify their betrayal afterwards? How did they explain this miracle away? When I left the mental hospital I was reminded of this story by the attitudes of some people in *my* life . . .

The Unbelievers

They do not believe me, I who have risen from the dead.
They sit in their sitting room, at dinner tables
Talking of this and that,
Seeing before their eyes the proof of my survival,
But when I have left the room, lean forward,
Suddenly quiet, and murmur confidentially,
"And how is she? How is she really?
Can she cope with the children, shopping, housework?
All the everyday cares of life?"
For they are the unbelievers
Doubtful of the daily struggle of rebirth.

Now Lazarus, he made them uncomfortable.
They sat in shadowed rooms talking, laughing,
An afternoon's belief lapsing into scepticism,
And when he rose and left the room, leant forward,
Suddenly quiet, to murmur confidentially,
"And how is Lazarus. How is he really?
No more pain, convulsions, comas?
No sign of further abnormality?"
"You are unbelievers" said Mary,
"He was dead and is no longer —
He stands before you living.
Can you doubt the miracles of God?"
She was, I think, a passionate woman.
And they of course, the betrayers,
Could not meet her eyes
But smiled and looked away.
They did not know what to make of him,
A number of reasons led them to Caiaphas.
Some had thought a miracle, some had not,
And of those who had been persuaded
Some felt they were mistaken,
Or it frightened them.
It was not they meant to be traitors,
Just the calm affirmation of recovery
Filled them with anxiety.
And so if Lazarus could not convince,
What little chance have I?
Bursting the gates of the asylum has nothing
To the drama of the tomb.
But years after, my little resurrection still disturbs.

Sarah

FRIENDSHIP WITH WOMEN

It seems strange now to think that until I had my first child and went into a therapeutic community I found it very difficult to communicate with other women; I felt I had nothing in common with them and certainly had no close women friends. I had no mothering as a child, what "affection" I had was from my father, inappropriate though it was. Women I associated with pain.

It was in the therapeutic community that I first learned to love a woman. I had a woman therapist and in effect she became my mother. She drew me out of a long darkness, held me, fed me and then allowed me to tantrum and play through childhood and adolescence until a year later I had grown enough to leave the hospital. The love and trust I felt for her allowed other relationships with women to grow, including, before her death, my real mother.

Gradually over the thirteen years since my community experience, my women friends have become more and more important to me — people to share my life with. Without their support I don't know how I would have worked out my feelings and experiences with my father. They have held me emotionally and, when I have needed it, physically.

In the first years after my husband left I knew that women were sustaining me, yet I still felt that this was second best; if I were truly worth something then I felt my husband would have wanted to stay with me. At last I have got to the point when I can ask myself whether a relationship with a man could give me what I share with my women friends — support, trust, companionship, honesty, love, freedom. It is not second best now to do things with other women — to see a film, go for a drink or to a party — but my first option. With them I can be both vulnerable and strong; in truth I can be myself, something no man has ever allowed me to be.

Sarah

About a women's group

I can't begin to speak of the immense growth I gained from an all women's group. It was a six month's course called Second Chance to Learn. With the love and support of the three tutors and each other, we looked back on our lives and reassessed them. Then together we shared painful experiences and developed a trust in each other. Through that we were able to go forward and gain the courage to take the next step into life.

We are still friends, and I am comforted by the knowledge that I am able to collapse in floods of tears or share in great joys too.

Susan

Friendship with women is something which can mean a lot to us personally. It also extends to a feeling of solidarity with women wherever they are.

Lady of the Night

Women of the streets, Ladies of the night,
You travel through bright lights and cars,
Cars of different numbers and colours.
How does it feel to meet the world?
Why do you go down those streets of pain?
It hurts me to see you weighed down by so many men and
with so much maleness.
You walk alone, but you carry so many.
I love all my sisters, you included.
Money to live, kids to feed, bills to pay.
The need to be loved.
We your sisters can fulfill all your needs. Let us help.
I'd like to put my arms around you and show you how much I care.
Take on some of your pain, soothe your bruised body.
Remove the faces of strangers from your mind and erase your fears.

Janet

OUR RIGHTS

When we started planning the book we decided that at the beginning we would need to describe the violence we had experienced, and the effect it had had on us. We knew that this would probably be painful both for us and the reader, but working on the list of rights printed below, helped us to keep up a spirit of optimism and hope while we were writing the more difficult parts of the book.

For women reading this book who are still in a violent situation, these rights may seem totally unrealistic – and to try to exercise them right now might be downright dangerous! Looking back though, to when we were in the same situation, we think they could have been a source of hope – something to hang on to and to think – "that's how I want my life to be". We think they might have helped us to realise that it wasn't always *us* who were in the wrong. After all if you've got a right to express an opinion or feeling, then it must be wrong to be abused for it.

Anyway, here is our list of rights – another group of women might have come up with something different – and readers might like to think up their own.

We have a right*

- To choose how to live our own lives – *e.g.* where we live, who we live with, whether to have children, how we express our sexuality.
- Not to be bound by everyone else's view of how we should behave.
- To be treated with respect as equal human beings.
- To express our opinions.
- To express our feelings – *e.g.* of anger or sadness.
- To be confident and courageous – or scared!
- To say yes and no for ourselves.
- Not to be responsible for *everyone* else *all* the time.
- To change our minds.
- To make mistakes.
- Not to feel guilty for *everything* that happens.
- To care for others and to share – both inside and outside a traditional family.
- To seek love – and to love ourselves.
- To have security and peace within ourselves.

* The idea of making a list of rights came from Anne Dickson's book on Assertiveness "A Woman in your own Right", and many of the rights we list are similar to hers.

We would like to end our book with this piece by Sarah, which expresses very well how we all feel.

When this group started the most important thing to me was coming to terms with what my father did to me as a child. I had to find some way of going through that experience and making some sense of it all. My childhood had blocked off great areas of my life; how to learn, how to experiment with learning, how to know what I wanted to know. I wanted to change all that. I wanted my life for me. This time was an exploration – a journey into myself and my own life.

Parallel with that developed relationships with the other women in the group. We are all so different, yet we found that we had so much in common. I learned to trust and love. I think, over this year, we have all changed and grown stronger.

Then the book became important to me. We have reached out in the group to each other. Somewhere out there, there are other women like us. I want to reach out to all those who are going through what we went through and share with them. Because we who have been abused are so many I can't hold you all in my arms, but the words I have written carry with them all the hope and love and strength I would like to give you. I want you to know that it is possible to change your lives, that it is hard and will take time, but it is possible.

CONTACT AND RESOURCES INFORMATION

The Women's Aid Federations which operation in England, Scotland, Northern Ireland and Wales offer advice, information, support and temporary accommodation in refuges for women and children suffering abuse.

They can be contacted at the addresses given below. They can put you in touch with your local refuge or if you want to get right away from your home locality, they can arrange to find you refuge in another part of the country.

CONTACT INFORMATION

Women's Aid Federation England Ltd. (W.A.F.E. Ltd)
PO Box 391
Bristol BS99 7WS
Admin and publication enquiries tel. *0272 633494*

W.A.F.E. National Helpline
Tel 0272 633542

W.A.F.E. operates a National Helpline for women seeking information, advice or refuge in England. It is open from 10 am to 10 pm (5 days a week, Mondays to Fridays). Outside these hours advice on how to get in touch with your local Women's Aid group is given on an ansaphone.

Referral to London refuges
via London Women's Aid Tel 071 251 6537

Northern Ireland Women's Aid
129 University Street
Belfast BT7 1HP
Tel 0232 249041 (office hours)

Welsh Women's Aid
38 - 48 Crwys Road
Cardiff CF2 4NN
Tel 0222 390874
(24 hour ansaphone with advice about referral to relevant agencies)

Welsh Women's Aid
12 Cambrian Place
Aberystwyth, Dyfed
Tel 0970 612748
(24 hour ansaphone with advice about referral to relevant agencies)

Scottish Women's Aid
13 North Bank Street
The Mound
Edinburgh EH3 6AG
Tel 031 225 8011
(24 hour telephone number given on ansaphone)

ASIAN WOMEN'S REFUGES

In England and Scotland there are several Asian Wome's Refuges where Asian women suffering violence can go with their children. You can contact them via the National Helpline in England or Scottish Women's Aid national office. Also agencies in your area, such as the Police, Social Services (Social Work Dept. in Scotland), Housing, and Samaritans may know if there is an Asian Women's Refuge in your area.

WOMEN'S AID PUBLICATIONS

All four of the Federations produce leaflets, books, posters and publish some books. For a current booklist and publication order form write to the Federations at the above addresses, a Self Addressed Envelope for the reply will be appreciated.